MW01199763

PASTA
RULES

DANILO CORTELLINI

PASTA RULES

100 Ways to Shape, Sauce, and Serve

Illustrations by
Rebecca Hollingsworth

UNION
SQUARE
& CO.

NEW YORK

UNION SQUARE & CO.

NEW YORK

UNION SQUARE & CO. and the distinctive Union Square & Co. logo are
trademarks of Sterling Publishing Co., Inc.

Union Square & Co., LLC, is a subsidiary of Sterling Publishing Co., Inc.

Text © 2025 Danilo Cortellini
Illustrations © 2025 Rebecca Hollingsworth

All rights reserved. No part of this publication may be reproduced, stored
in a retrieval system, or transmitted in any form or by any means (including
electronic, mechanical, photocopying, recording, or otherwise) without prior
written permission from the publisher.

ISBN 978-1-4549-5698-3
ISBN 978-1-4549-5699-0 (e-book)

Library of Congress Control Number: 2024950028

For information about custom editions, special sales, and premium purchases,
please contact specialsales@unionsquareandco.com.

Printed in China

2 4 6 8 10 9 7 5 3 1

unionsquareandco.com

Cowriter: Kaltrina Bylykbashi
Editor: Caitlin Leffel
Designer: Renée Bollier
Illustrator: Rebecca Hollingsworth
Project Editor: Ivy McFadden
Production Manager: Terence Campo
Copy Editor: Kerry Acker

Shutterstock.com: Alina Beketova: throughout (pasta headers);
mything: 6-7

To my nonna and my mamma,
for teaching me that the best way to keep a
family together through life's challenges is
sharing meals. And to my wife and kids, for
the constant support and joy.

TABLE OF CONTENTS

INTRODUCTION

Creating a list of definitive rules about pasta is like trying to herd cats. As a chef of twenty years and a born-and-bred Italian, I know that some pasta fundamentals should be followed to get the best out of every dish. But there are so many vastly differing opinions about what's right and what's wrong that the minute you make one claim, you contradict another. Pasta is incredibly unifying in its popularity but also the subject of sharply divisive debate—both among the regions of Italy and across international waters.

If you want to understand the tight parameters we're working within, take the tortellini versus cappelletti debate, which I cover in chapter 2 (Rule 27). Two pasta shapes distinguished by the smallest differences are vehemently defended by opposing sides of Emilia-Romagna in northern Italy. Some argue that the size of the central cavity differentiates the shapes, others the sauces with which they are served. Most would not know whether they have been served one or the other. Who needs Montagues versus Capulets when you have indistinguishable belly button–shaped pasta to argue about?

Needless to say, we Italians take pasta very seriously. It has become inextricably linked with our identity. We cook, we eat, and we preach about pasta every day. Perhaps because of this, there is a growing group we can call the "traditionalists" who have taken it upon themselves to become a sort of pasta police. A menace on social media (I have received many comments from them myself), great arbiters in their restaurants, and the most brilliant of pontificators, these personalities will be the first to point out what's "authentically" Italian and what's not. Snapping spaghetti?

A hard no. Using cream in sauces? Absolutely not. Cooking pasta until it's mushy? Forget about it. I admit I have affection for these curmudgeonly characters. I am Italian, after all. We have become protective of our traditions over the years as globalization, commercialization, and migration spread our word across the world and returned it to us unrecognizable. These people are passionate and they are knowledgeable. But are they always right? No. Authenticity is largely an imagined myth. While one end of Italy may be stubbornly against a perceived act against pasta, the other will welcome it wholeheartedly. I am guilty of endorsing and breaking my own rules in equal measure.

So why trust the rules of a guy who thoroughly enjoys bending them? Because I'd like to offer a third way: some gentle guidelines to make it easier for you to traverse the world of pasta from the perspective of an Italian who doesn't take the rules too seriously. I want to help you differentiate between a technical rule that will actually make your pasta better (like not overcooking your pasta) and a cultural preference that may have only emerged in recent decades (fish and cheese might go together, after all). Think of this book as your passport to our biggest cultural ticks, so that you'll know how to hold your own in the kitchen, at a restaurant, when traveling, or when invited into an Italian home.

I love Italy. I love its traditions, its cuisine, and especially its people. It inspires me daily because it's reflected through my family, my friends, and the many creative people making great food across the country. I would like others to see Italy the way I see it, and the best way to do this is through pasta.

IT ALL
STARTS WITH
DOUGH

The very essence of pasta is dough. It's the foundation from which count-less types of pasta variations, shapes, and dishes are built, whether it be fresh egg pasta tortellini plunged into a warming broth, or dried semolina rigatoni served in a satiating combination of guanciale, pecorino, and tomatoes. Knowing your dough gives you a peek into Italy's regional differences: why you get Apulian orecchiette, Roman fettuccine, Tuscan pappardelle, and Sicilian casarecce. It will also give you an appreciation for what makes each pasta variety unique. If you plan on going hands-first into shaping your own pasta or you're simply gathering information to order your next dish, dough is the very first step.

Italian DNA is not a prerequisite for excellent dough-making. I grew up with the advantage of watching my nonna and mamma making fresh pasta, but it wasn't until I finished cooking school and started working in a fresh pasta restaurant in Verona that I began to understand the crucial dif-ferences between dough for ravioli, tagliatelle, and lasagne. As there are

hundreds of varieties of pasta in Italy, you learn as you go, and practice makes perfect. Here, I will be giving you the tools to help you identify not only what to look out for but also to feel for.

When it comes to dough, you do have to follow some rigid rules, but once you've mastered these basics, you can go wild with experimentation. Traditionalists will have a lot to say about all of this and many regions of Italy even have protected recipes that proclaim a Bolognese a true Bolognese, or a carbonara a true carbonara. But I think people should be given room to play—albeit within certain parameters. I love playing with colored pasta, and I love to experiment with different flour combinations to achieve that perfect texture and finish. In this sense, I think having fun is a must when taking on pasta from scratch. So, while the following may not be definitive rules, they are what I believe to be the most important considerations for pasta dough-making.

Ready, Set, Dough: Prep Your Workspace

Chefs call it mise en place, others call it thinking ahead or getting organized—whatever the terminology, preparation is essential to making perfect fresh pasta dough. Picture an Italian nonna, the counter free of clutter, kneading away like she's part of a production line. Be that nonna.

To begin, lay out your ingredients, with some spare on hand in case of any mishaps. If the dough is too sticky, you might need to quickly add a touch of flour to get it just right. If your dough becomes dry and crumbly, that extra splash of egg or water will save the day.

When describing their recipes, seasoned Italian home cooks like my discerning mother will offer vague advice like, "Use enough eggs for the proportion of flour." That's because a more experienced cook will be able to produce a balanced dough just by the feel of it, but there is no shame in getting the scales out and measuring ingredients, including the eggs.

DANILO SAYS . . .

Your work surface needs to be free of objects so nothing gets in the way when you're kneading and rolling out dough, especially for long pasta like tagliatelle or pappardelle.

Tune Into Dough's Delicate Dance

Dough-making is not an exact science. Hand temperature, work surface, air circulation in the room, and humidity will all have an impact on the dough's water content, and therefore how much extra flour, water, or egg you may need to get the texture just right. The aim is to always be in control of the dough's moisture levels.

The work surface is one area where I am a purist: I believe there is no better surface on which to work your dough than a wooden board. Traditionally used by families all over Italy, wooden boards are porous and suck up additional moisture from dough as you knead, preventing the likelihood of "wet" dough. Though they are less welcome in professional kitchens (in large part due to stricter hygiene rules), at home I still use a special pasta board that's rectangular and much longer than a typical cutting board. While you can work on a range of surfaces, from stainless-steel tables to marble counters, be aware that most surfaces are stickier than wood and will therefore require more flour, which will be absorbed into the dough and, if you're not careful, could result in denser pasta.

Surface properties combined with the room's atmosphere can make or break pasta dough. Pasta hates humidity, so damp basements are a no-go. A well-ventilated space will mean pasta doesn't stick to your hands or tools. But be warned that a windy space can dry pasta too quickly, making it crumbly and difficult to shape.

Good Dough Takes Time

Showing dough a little love and patience is key to creating the tastiest pasta. This is particularly true when it comes to folding all the ingredients together and massaging them into the perfect texture. The more time spent palming the dough, stretching and pulling it back together, the more its gluten will develop and activate, binding it into a smooth, supple ball. Unlike with the process of making bread, it's technically impossible to overknead pasta dough.

Whether kneading is done by hand or a stand mixer is an ongoing source of family feuds all over Italy, but both are acceptable in my opinion. I prefer the more romantic method of kneading by hand, but I have nothing against a mixer, which saves effort when making big batches. It's what I use most in a professional kitchen because it mimics the movements and gestures of hands. A mixer creates results that are just as good in roughly 5 minutes, whereas with hands you'd be working the dough for about 15 minutes.

DANILO SAYS . . .

I would try to avoid using a food processor for this stage. While it takes just 2 minutes to "knead" and I have tried it with okay(ish) results, I find that the resulting dough is too soft and loses structure because of the aggressive blade. That said, in the spirit of keeping a distance from definitive statements: Use it if it's all that is available to you.

Siesta! Resting Dough Is Essential

Rest will totally transform your dough. Freshly kneaded dough is smooth, elastic, and bounces back, making it difficult to work with. This dough would not hold its shape or roll out into a sheet, folding back like the coils of a tight spring. With rest, dough relaxes and loses its edge, and a gluten mesh forms, making it pliable and easy to mold. Rest is when the wet and dry ingredients really become one. Poke the dough before and after rest to compare how much it fights back.

If you want to use the dough right away, the quickest, easiest way to rest it is to put it in a bowl, cover it with plastic wrap, and let it stand at room temperature for 30 minutes. If you're using it later in the day, store it in the fridge—though I don't recommend refrigerating it any longer than overnight (see Rule 6). Traditionally, some would rest pasta with a cloth or towel draped over it, but as this is not airtight, it can dry out the surface of the dough, which you will have to trim off. To reduce your plastic use, airtight containers, reusable resealable bags, and vacuum-pack storage all work— or do as my mamma did: Place the dough on a wooden board and cover it with a bowl.

Break It Down (One Step at a Time)

Whether you're making water-based pasta or egg-based pasta, pasta shaped like little ears or big tubes or small parcels, the key to rolling out dough is to take it one step at a time. It doesn't matter if your tool of choice is a traditional rolling pin or a stainless-steel pasta maker: It's essential to work gradually from a thick piece of rested dough to the desired width of your pasta sheet.

Lightly flour your work surface and slice the dough into smaller pieces so that it's easier to work with. Flatten the first slice of dough with your hands and cover the rest with plastic wrap or a dishcloth so it doesn't dry out. (Alternatively, you can keep the remaining dough in a resealable bag while you work each portion.) Work the dough with a rolling pin to reach your desired thickness, whether that's completely by hand, or just enough to fit it into a pasta machine. It's good practice to fold back your pasta sheet into itself initially and then start again; this reintegrates "nerve" in the pasta that has lost its elasticity. While you're rolling, remember to only dust it with extra flour if it sticks to your hands or the work surface.

Many recipes will say a good pasta sheet needs to be so thin that it almost becomes translucent. But that's only applicable when you're making a shape that requires thin pasta sheets. Take spaghetti alla chitarra from my home region in Abruzzo: A thick, robust noodle shape up to 3 millimeters thick, it is made to perfectly catch the region's hearty sauces. So think of the context of your pasta, why you're making it, and what purpose it serves, and you will arrive at the density you need.

Fresh Dough Is the Best Dough

Once you've taken the time to make dough from scratch, don't be tempted to cheat at the last hurdle by freezing it for later. Nor should you make it days before it will be eaten.

Fresh pasta dough is easier to manage and will give you the best results. A pasta dough that has been stored for too long in the fridge becomes soft and sticky because it releases humidity. If it's refrigerated for 24 hours or more, it oxidizes and becomes a paler, grayish color.

But this shouldn't mean that you need to be making fresh pasta just ahead of a major family event or a dinner party with friends. The trick is to dry, freeze, or refrigerate pasta once it has already been shaped.

Know Your Dough(s)!

Pasta is not homogenous. Many types of pasta steadily developed across different regions of Italy—and indeed the world—over time. These variants are a direct result of dough being treated dissimilarly: what goes in it along with how it's combined and cooked. So the rule here is to be aware that there are variances among doughs: different flours, doughs with egg, and doughs without. Covering every type of dough is a book unto itself, but in the following rules, I share what I believe to be the essentials.

First Things First: The Flour

Two types of flour make up the majority of pasta dough: durum wheat flour (or semolina) and soft wheat flour. Most commonly, coarser durum wheat flours are used for dried pasta, which is made simply with water and flour, while softer, more finely milled flours are used for fresh pasta made with egg. The former is more suited to extruded shapes and those that need to hold their form when cooked, like rigatoni, penne, and macaroni, whereas the latter is ideal for shapes that require more flexibility or foldability, like tagliatelle and tortellini. However, as always with Italian cuisine, this is not a definitive rule. In Tuscany, for example, there is pici pasta (see Rule 39), made from 0 flour, a soft wheat flour, water, and olive oil. In Italy, 00 (or doppio zero) flour is the most regularly used soft wheat flour, and internationally this is often referred to as "pasta flour." The difference between 00 flour and 0 flour is that 00 flour is more refined (it's sifted and finely milled) and therefore needs less liquid when kneading. All-purpose flour can be substituted for either.

Eggless Dough: Knead to Succeed

The very first pasta dough that was ever made was most likely eggless. Eggs were an expensive commodity in the twelfth century, when pasta began to take the form we know and love today, which means that most people were eating pasta made from just flour and water. Southern Italy is particularly known for this type of pasta and the vast majority of pasta in stores is made with eggless dough.

Eggless pasta is most commonly made from a type of durum wheat flour that we call *semola rimacinata* ("semola milled twice"). It's similar to what you might know as semolina but with a finer grind. Compared to plain flour from soft wheat, semola has a more vibrant yellow color and contains more protein and fiber. There are other differences: It's coarse and lends more texture and a rustic feel to the pasta. Its sturdy disposition is why you get the grooves in your rigatoni or lines in your penne. It also absorbs more liquid during dough-making and more sauce when prepared.

To form an eggless dough, you pretty much follow the steps above: Mix the water with the flour, a little pinch of salt, and a drizzle of extra-virgin

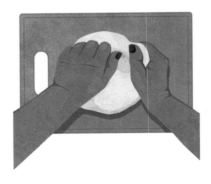

olive oil. Get on with the kneading, stretching, and pulling until you achieve a smooth, elastic dough. The rule to remember here is that dough made from semola needs to be worked for longer when kneading; see the recipe in Rule 19.

Semola rimacinata dough is the one occasion where (almost) everybody in Italy agrees you should add olive oil to the pasta dough. Though it isn't essential, a touch of olive oil gives you more elasticity and a more fluid dough. It also gives you a nice flavor on top of helping to shape the pasta. This kind of dough works best for short pasta shapes like cavatelli, orecchiette, gnocchetti, and fusilli.

Egg-Based Dough: Made to Be Measured

Fresh egg pasta is the most common variety made at home, and probably the one that most people are referring to when they speak about making pasta. It is that much more special because it's less common in stores than its dry durum wheat flour counterpart.

Fresh egg pasta hails from the north of Italy, where soft wheat flour has been cultivated historically because of its cooler climate. Soft wheat flour is lower in nutrients than durum wheat flour and has a higher sugar content as it is more refined, but on the upside, it's much more common and easier to work with. When this type of flour is combined with egg, it produces a dough that is rich in flavor, golden in color, and silky in texture.

Egg pasta can be easier to make as it takes a little less elbow grease to get a smooth texture and all you have to do is combine the ingredients in a simple ratio: The flour weight should be double that of the eggs. Otherwise, the same basic rules of pasta dough-making apply here, too (see Rule 18). Another benefit is that the dough can be used for almost any shape you want to cook up.

My main advice regarding egg pasta is to mind the eggs. Experienced pasta makers like the *sfoglinas* of Emilia-Romagna will say one egg for every 100 grams of flour. But eggs come in all sizes. A person with experience and practice will add more flour when the consistency doesn't feel right, but someone new to pasta-making can struggle to get this right by touch. Always weigh your eggs along with the flour.

All-Yolk Dough: Handle with Care

Another one from the north of Italy, yolk-only pasta originated in Piedmont. The most famous type of pasta made with only yolks and flour are tagliolini (known as tajarin in Piedmont): thick strips of rich yellow noodles. Though this type of dough is usually made with 00 flour, some cooks like to add a little semola, too; but what sets it apart from regular pasta is that the egg whites aren't used.

What happens to dough made from yolks only? The dough is more rigid and harder to work, but the finish is silky and bright in color. This is because yolks and whites do different things to your dough. Egg whites are mostly water—nearly 90 percent of egg white is water—while the egg yolk is made up of around 50 percent water mixed with fats and proteins. Less diluted, the yolks give deeper color and richness to the dough but less hydration. This brings me to my rule about yolk-only pasta: Watch the moisture level. With less water content, the dough will need extra care so that it doesn't dry out and remains pliable.

Also, the whole-egg pasta rule of doubling the amount of the egg to flour doesn't work here. In my opinion, the best results come from measuring

about 650 grams of yolk for each kilo of 00 flour, but as mentioned, be ready to adapt as you knead if needed. A traditional recipe from Piedmont calls for 40 eggs for each kilo of 00 flour (conveniently named "the 40-egg dough"). But even here, there are disputes as some recipes call for 30 yolks. Both are likely right. Remember: Not all eggs are the same size.

This dough is so rich and silky that I find myself using it more often than whole-egg dough when cooking at home. However, it does have its limitations and isn't recommended for pasta shapes that need a lot of molding. It's great for lasagne, tagliatelle, and pappardelle, but less so if you're making ravioli, tortellini, or anything that is folded and sealed.

Yolk-only pasta is usually served with very simple sauces because it is already rich. In Piedmont, a local specialty is tajarin al tartufo, a sumptuous dish of silky pasta coated in butter and topped with truffle. When the pasta is cut very thin, it's also served in broth.

Give Enriched Eggs a Try

Pasta makers and chefs across the world are increasingly using enriched-yolk eggs to achieve a brighter color or more luxurious flavor. These yolks become enriched by changing the diet of the chicken and feeding them a corn-based diet or additional beta-carotene and supplements—and not, as I embarrassingly believed for too long, by letting chickens roam freely under the Italian sun. I highly recommend the use of these eggs for yolk-only pasta, as they add so much flavor to a dish.

Take It Back: Reclaim Whole Wheat Dough

From the mother of all grains, whole wheat flour is an ancient ingredient, used for millennia. In reality, all pasta was probably made from this type of flour at one point, which is why I consider this a classic pasta, even if it isn't the most common. The past fifteen years have seen a big wave of health-conscious chefs return to these grains for their full flavor and impressive nutrient profile.

Less refined than its more modern counterparts, whole wheat flour—as its name suggests—uses the entirety of the seed, including the bran and germ, in its composition. It's coarser than 00 flour, has a brownish tint, and contains lots of protein, vitamins, and fiber. This contributes to a hearty flavor and the rough texture common in rustic dishes.

Dough made from whole wheat flour is not as pliable and can be slightly crumblier than that made of 00 flour due to its reduced gluten content. This makes it a little harder to work and combine, but the flavor payoff is worth it. Aside from this, the steps are the same as above, whether you're using water or eggs.

DANILO SAYS . . .

I turn to this dough when I'm craving pasta but also want to feel like a grown-up who makes healthy choices. The best of both worlds.

Gnocchi Is Pasta

This is a controversial one. But if you ask me, anything containing flour is technically a dough. Italian food historian Luca Cesari has shown that cookbooks have referred to gnocchi as pasta since the Renaissance period—or by the word often used for pasta at the time, *maccheroni*. Gnocchi actually predate the arrival of potatoes to Italy; one of the first recipes for gnocchi was recorded in the fourteenth century and was made with fresh cheese, egg yolks, and flour.

Today, the version made with potato is the most widely known, but gnocchi is its own category of pasta with its own offshoots of shapes and contents. It can be made with pumpkin, eggplant, ricotta, and more.

Making gnocchi dough is not so different from making colored pasta dough, as the proportions of ingredients are similarly inverted. For a basic gnocchi recipe, potato becomes the dominant ingredient and is mixed with a much smaller amount of flour and a dash of egg. The flour here is used to bind ingredients together rather than being the main event; the potato is the star of the show.

As with any pasta dough, no matter what type of gnocchi you're making, remember to control the moisture. Make sure you drain as much liquid as possible from your ingredients. Pumpkin should drain overnight in the fridge, preferably under some kind of weight that pushes all the liquid out. You can drain potatoes in a clean dishcloth, then pat them dry before you mix them with flour and egg.

DANILO SAYS . . .

Bread gnocchi deserve a special mention here. Yes, you read that right; there are a string of gnocchi look-alikes made with breadcrumbs or rehydrated stale bread instead of flour. Born out of the need to use up leftovers, bread gnocchi are often characterized as a *primo piatto* (first course) on Italian menus together with pasta and rice. You can find bread gnocchi as passatelli in Emilia-Romagna, or canederli in Trentito–South Tyrol. Though bread gnocchi aren't considered pasta by most, I'm willing to go against the grain and put them in the gnocchi family.

Welcome Gluten-Free Pasta

Intolerances are sometimes softly ridiculed, and catering to the various special diets seen in today's world—dairy-free, nut-free, meat-free—can be difficult for chefs. But I find the fact that so many people want to experiment with and enjoy different types of pasta quite exciting. And with the growing global love for this type of food, it's wonderful to see that people are finding new approaches that include everyone.

In the past, Italians who couldn't tolerate gluten simply didn't eat pasta if their intolerance was severe (if you can imagine such a thing!) or eat it less often if it meant dealing with some bloating afterward. But now we have the tools, awareness, and knowledge to produce gluten-free pasta dough. Recipes have been adapted, and cooks have changed their habits when necessary.

There's no doubt that making gluten-free pasta presents a challenge. Gluten is what holds the dough together and makes it pliable and chewy. Once the gluten is removed, dough can lack elasticity and take on a hard quality. So, to overcome this, we have to find alternative ingredients that have similar properties. Today, people commonly use gluten-free flours with added xantham gum to replicate gluten's glue-like texture. But we can also look to the past for ideas. Rice flour, used to make noodles for centuries across Asia, works well for pasta because its starch re-creates gluten's stickiness. Elsewhere, carob flour—which is rich in protein and has been used as a thickener and emulsifier for gelato in some parts of Italy—has been used in the past in conjunction with semola in Sicily to create cavatelli. Buckwheat flour, more popular in the north of Italy, is another gluten-free option. Take the recipe for pizzoccheri hailing from Valtellina in Lombardy; it calls for a small amount of regular flour, but you can simply substitute rice flour. Just take care when forming the dough with alternatives because it can be crumblier than regular wheat flour.

Make It Your Own

Traditionalists may scoff, but here's why getting people to experiment with different flours and dough recipes is important to me: I believe that the more you play and practice, paying attention to how different variables affect your dough, the more you will learn what dough works best for you and the recipe you're making. This spirit of experimentation is part of what brought regional variances—and hundreds of types of pasta—into existence in the first place. This is the main reason our favorite recipes developed from town to town, family to family. Each is tweaked for particular tastes and customs.

In my experience, the best dough is the one you mix with the type of flour that achieves the best result for what you want to create. I like to combine a larger percentage of 00 flour with about 30 percent of durum wheat for longer pasta like tagliatelle, pappardelle, tagliolini, or spaghetti to give more body and flavor to the pasta. Elsewhere I might add a little water or extra egg yolk to liquid ingredients to enhance or dilute certain flavors for pasta like ceppe Abruzzesi. Once you've learned the basic rules, push the limits. Pasta is not a perfect science—that's the beauty of it.

Splash the Color (When the Occasion Calls)

Colored pasta has finally gotten a seat at the table, with some pros making an art form of their incredible, intricate designs. I have been fascinated by colored pasta dough since I was a little kid, and as soon as I started my career, I couldn't wait to work with it. I was completely enraptured by colorful dishes: green and yellow tagliatelle paglia e fieno ("straw and hay pasta"), lasagne verdi, and spaghetti al nero, which is made with squid ink.

To make colored dough, you follow the general rules of fresh pasta (see Rule 18) but add additional ingredients to make the rainbow: saffron for bright yellow, beetroot for pink, and boiled spinach for green. You do need to figure out how these additional ingredients are going to affect the dough. When using wet ingredients like spinach and beetroot, subtract the weight of the ingredients from the weight of liquids (eggs or water). So, for example, if the original recipe calls for 100 grams of eggs and 200 grams of flour, you can use 50 grams of eggs, 50 grams of the wet ingredients, and knead it in with the flour. The opposite is true for the addition of dry, colored ingredients. If, for example, you want to make cocoa pasta ("Sacrilege!" some might say, but trust me, it is not as sweet as you might imagine; see Rule 93), you can add 100 grams of eggs, 150 grams of flour, and 50 grams of unsweetened cocoa powder. Don't be afraid to get creative—my biggest tip here is to be brave and experiment widely.

DANILO SAYS . . .

I stay away from food coloring because fresh ingredients do the trick but with an added benefit: They add flavor. The flavor is subtle, but it builds layers of taste and depth to a dish that synthetic coloring can't replicate.

 18

Perfect Fresh Egg Pasta Dough

Serves 4

400g 00 flour or all-purpose flour, plus more for dusting
200g whole eggs (about 4 large eggs)

On a clean work surface or in a bowl, create a volcano-like crater with the flour and drop in the eggs. Beat the eggs with a fork and gradually incorporate the flour. When the ingredients start to bind together, begin kneading with your hands. (Remember that during this step it's important to stretch and pull your dough while kneading to allow the flour's gluten to start forming). After a few minutes of kneading, it will slowly come together and result in a smooth and homogeneous dough. If your dough feels too sticky, add a pinch of flour; if it's too dry and not binding, you can add a touch of egg or even a splash of water.

When you've finished kneading, wrap your dough in plastic wrap and let rest at room temperature for 30 minutes.

Using a rolling pin or pasta maker, roll the dough into pasta sheets. (The size will depend on the pasta you are making.) If you have a wooden board, that's great; if you don't, any clean surface will work (see Rule 1). Cut the pasta into thick sheets and flatten them with a rolling pin or with the help of a pasta machine. (It's good practice to fold your rolled pasta over itself and repeat a couple of times; this process will give you a smooth rectangular sheet that will be easier to work with at a later stage.)

If you're using a pasta machine, gradually work from the largest to narrowest settings to make pasta sheets suitable to your intended shape. Let your pasta sheets dry for 5 minutes on your board before cutting it into any shapes and remember to dust with extra flour only if it feels sticky.

19

Hone an Eggless Pasta Recipe

Serves 4

500g semola rimacinata flour (see Rule 9)
300ml warm water (about 1¼ cups)
1 to 2 teaspoons extra-virgin olive oil (optional)
Pinch of salt
Flour, for dusting

On a clean work surface or in a bowl, mix the water with the oil (if using) and salt. Gradually incorporate the flour. When the ingredients start to bind together, start kneading with your hands. (Remember that during this step it's important to stretch and pull your dough while kneading to allow the flour's gluten to start working.) After a few minutes of kneading, it will slowly come together and result in a smooth and homogeneous dough. If your dough feels too sticky, add a pinch of flour; if it's too dry and not binding, you can add a splash of water.

When you're finished kneading, wrap your dough in plastic wrap and let rest at room temperature for 30 minutes.

This dough is usually made to create "tool-free" pasta shapes like cavatelli, so you can even avoid the rolling part and move directly to shaping. You'll find more details in chapter 2.

Go All-Yolk

Serves 2 or 3

200g 00 or all-purpose flour, plus more for dusting
50g semola rimacinata flour (see Rule 9)
170g egg yolks (about 8 large yolks)

The traditional way of making yolk-only pasta is with 00 flour, but I tend to add a smaller percentage of semola to obtain a firmer texture.

Either way, the steps are pretty much the same as any egg-based dough: You beat the egg yolks and incorporate the flour gradually with a fork; when it starts to bind, you knead by hand until you have a smooth and elastic dough; and as always, be ready with a touch of flour or extra yolks (liquid) to adjust if needed.

TAKING
SHAPE

The shape of the pasta is a major indicator of the type of dish you are about to enjoy. You likely have become accustomed to certain forms paired with specific sauces: penne with spicy tomato, spaghetti with garlic and olive oil, orzo in chicken broth. But with hundreds of shapes to consider, and slight variations promoted by Italy's villages, towns, and regions—let alone what you find on your local grocery store shelf—it's hard to know how to start picking a shape and what to serve it with. So how did these pasta shapes come to be? Why were they created? And what sauce, broth, meat, or spice should they be paired with? It would be a mammoth task to know every type—I doubt anyone knows every pasta shape that's ever existed. However, there are some key tips and tricks that can help you understand the many forms we have today.

We have already discussed how dough impacts shape; that fresh eggs with soft wheat flour are more likely to make a foldable tortellini because of the dough's flexibility, while eggless dough with semolina flour is more

likely to work for a Southern Italian dish like orecchiette. But whatever the outcome, to go from dough to shape, one of three methods will be employed: the dough will either be rolled into a flat sheet, cut into a nugget and massaged into shape by hand, or extruded through a die in a machine (or an attachment on your pasta maker). Flat sheets, most likely made from egg dough, can become a multitude of shapes from lasagna sheets to ravioli. Hand-shaped pasta made from semolina and water means gnocchetti Sardi or cavatelli. The hard shapes like bucatini or penne will usually be mass-produced by a machine. If I were a beginner, I wouldn't invest in an extrusion tool because it's expensive and takes a little more effort to get right, but it may be something you consider as you get more confident.

Learn the 6 Pasta "Food Groups"

As general guidance, here are six categories that I use to help identify certain families of pasta:

- **Long pasta (*pasta lunga*):** Any pasta you need to twist with a fork to get a mouthful. There's the more common spaghetti and linguine, but also those of varying diameters like chitarra, bigoli, or pici.

- **Short pasta (*pasta corta*):** This includes a wide breadth of shapes that are simply cut to suit a forkful; all other rules about them vary. They may be made using all kinds of dough, come from all parts of Italy, and can be dressed in a wide range of sauces. Think of spirals of fusilli, bow-shaped farfalle, ear-shaped orecchiette, and so on. Short shapes made from egg-based dough tend to be a little rarer than the widely manufactured short, dry shapes like penne, fusilli, and rigatoni. Many such shapes, like garganelli, farfalle, and sorpresine, are from the north, which we know because they are made using egg-based dough made with 00 flour (see Rule 10). These shapes were developed in response to a lack of resources at the time that they were created. Short pasta from the south of Italy is usually made from a little nugget of dough. The oldest of them is cavatelli (see Rule 33), and you'll find that (almost) every recipe relates to the original technique of this shape.

- **Pasta nests (*pasta in nido*):** Strands of pasta that are laid and gathered in a circular shape when dried, like tagliatelle, pappardelle, fettuccine, and capelli d'angelo (or "angel hair"). Each nest is usually a serving for one.

- **Tiny pasta (*pastina*):** Small shapes measuring a couple of centimeters or less are often referred to as pastina, which are used in broths and soups. Some examples include quadrucci, filini, anelli—and even pasta mista, which is a variety of leftover pasta shapes thrown together into soup.

- **Pasta tubes (*pasta a tubo*):** A wide variety of pasta is a tubular shape with a hollow middle; think of strands of bucatini, large tubes of paccheri, quills of penne, or small curves of macaroni. These are almost always created with an extrusion machine, so they aren't commonly made at home, but they tend to be the ones you find on supermarket shelves.

- **Weird and wonderful:** Some regional pasta shapes don't categorize well. They require unusual techniques to get their shape and are incredibly characteristic of their area, city, town, or even family. These are covered in Rules 38–41.

Get Acquainted with Italy's North-South Divide

Italy's local traditions dictate much of what happens to pasta. Understanding some of the differences between the north and south can help you categorize how a specific shape of pasta should be made or dressed.

Generally speaking, pasta made from soft wheat and eggs comes from the north (see Rule 10). Here, pasta shapes are now most commonly made with a pasta machine or rolling pin, so you find forms that begin their life as a flat sheet, like tagliatelle, lasagna, tagliolini, or garganelli. These are often prepared with butter-based or meat-based sauces; ragù Bolognese from Bologna, cacio e pepe from Rome, or tagliolini al tartufo from Piedmont.

In the south, you more typically find water-based dough with semolina shaped by hand from little nuggets of dough. These little nuggets are formed into shapes like orecchiette, cavatelli, or gnocchetti Sardi, and then dressed in lighter sauces, lots of olive oil, tomatoes, vegetables, and fish, like cavatelli cozze e fagioli from Puglia, busiate alla Trapanese from Sicily, or gnocchetti Sardi alla Carlofortina.

These regional pasta traditions largely evolved from playing with what was locally available. Surrounded by France, Switzerland, and Austria, the north has Alpine influences with common pairings including cheeses and game. The south is mostly coastal so you'll find an abundance of seafood, tomatoes, and vegetables. Take the dish orecchiette con le cime di rapa from Bari. This dish would have come about because cime di rapa (turnip greens) grow in the region of Puglia where Bari is located. And the orecchiette shape was developed in the south, where pasta is often served with oils and vegetables that each tiny cup perfectly catches. This is a quintessential example of a dish that's very typical of the south, down to the produce it's served with.

As always, there will be outliers. Pici, a thick noodle-shaped pasta, is made from water-based dough and comes from the north. Trofie, the rolled short sticks also from the north, are made from eggless dough rolled from a small nugget. Central Italy often has influences from both north and south, as well as its own specialties, like chestnut flour dough. While we Italians made the traditions, we have also been some of the first to break them—and this has formed the ever-evolving story of pasta.

DANILO SAYS . . .

If you're making fresh pasta for the first time, here are some inexpensive tools I'd recommend to make your pasta-making journey easier:

- **Rolling pin:** Even if you have nothing else, a rolling pin is essential to get a flat pasta sheet; but, then again, you could use a Saran Wrap roll or a bottle of wine.

- **Dough scraper:** This all-in-one tool is useful both in the kneading process—when it helps to efficiently remove excessive dough from your surface—and for shaping forms like gnocchi when you cut the nuggets into shape.

- **Pasta cutter:** A wheel-shaped utensil with a smooth or ridged texture used to cut homemade dough into shapes; what you would use to cut the ragged edges of ravioli.

- **Ring-shaped cookie cutters:** These will help you create perfect circles for certain shapes like cappellacci or tortelloni—and you're likely to need one for pastries at some point.

- **Pastry brush:** A small brush that's great for applying liquids to dough. (I'll admit at home I use paint brushes because they're better made and more resistant.)

Lasagne: Pasta Sheets That Support Heavy Sauce

Lasagna is one of the oldest pasta dishes, dating as far back as the Middle Ages. Its name alludes to its age as the word *lasagna* is said to come from the ancient Greek word for flatbread, *laganon*. Hailing from Emilia-Romagna, lasagna sheets (known as *sfoglia*) are made from an egg-based dough typical of the region. A large flat sheet is rolled by hand or using a machine and cut into rectangular sections that will then be layered with cheese and sauce.

To ensure your sheets are durable enough to support the sauce, I recommend you roll the dough to roughly 1.5 millimeters thick, dust it with flour, and let it dry on a work surface or a wooden board for 5 minutes on each side. Then roll it again to create a stretched effect so that the sheets are porous and absorb more sauce.

Get to Know a Handmade Pasta Tube

Cannelloni is one of the few tubular forms you can shape at home. Following a similar process to lasagne, each cannelloni is made from a square sheet of pasta dough that is filled and folded to create a cylinder. Cannelloni has become popular all over Italy because it's versatile and can be filled with a range of ingredients, most commonly with ricotta and spinach or minced meat. The shape is relatively new compared to some of the forms we will speak about, with the first recipe of cannelloni di pasta having been recorded in a book by Alberto Cougnet called *L'arte Cucinaria in Italia* in 1910.

To make cannelloni, cut a flat pasta sheet into squares of 10 to 15 centimeters (4 to 6 inches), then use a pastry bag or spoon to place a line of filling along the middle of each square. Roll the pasta around the filling until it overlaps and connects on its opposite end. Brush the edges with water to help seal them together. Once this is done, place the cannelloni in a baking dish, dress with a traditional tomato or béchamel sauce, sprinkle with cheese, then bake until golden.

 25

Nidi di Rondine: Make Room for Error

Nidi di rondine is the swirled pasta form meant to resemble a swallow's nest—its namesake. This too is made from a large flat sheet of egg-based pasta that is rolled with fillings of cheese, prosciutto, or mushrooms. Here, unlike with cannelloni, the filling is spread all over the sheet before it's rolled like a roulade, which is then sliced into thick 4- to 5-centimeter (1½- to 2-inch) segments. The long rolls are then placed upright in a buttered dish, covered in béchamel sauce, and cooked in the oven until golden. Said to come from the microstate San Marino in the Emilia-Romagna region, it can be found across Italy, especially in the north.

When making this shape, I'd recommend you create as large a pasta sheet as possible to leave room for error. Like with lasagne, the thickness of the sheet is important; it should be about 1.5 millimeters. Avoid overfilling so you don't struggle with rolling it into shape.

DANILO SAYS . . .

When I make lasagna or cannelloni with freshly made pasta sheets, I don't boil them first (as tradition dictates) but instead use them as they are. It's quicker, but keep in mind they will absorb more sauce than preboiled pasta when baked in the oven. Keep sauces a little thinner if you want to follow my method.

 26

The Holy Trinity of Nested Pasta: Pay Attention to Small Yet Important Size Differences

About 1 centimeter separates three very popular nested pasta forms: pappardelle, tagliatelle, and fettuccine. Made much in the same way, all three shapes require you to bring together fresh egg dough, roll, then create a flat rectangular pasta sheet. This sheet is then floured and folded into itself, bringing the longer edges to the center so they meet in the middle. The distinction between the shapes is in how wide you cut the strips from there, allowing for a strip 5 millimeters wide for fettuccine, between 5 and 10 millimeters for tagliatelle, and nearly 2 centimeters wide for pappardelle.

There is such a similarity between these shapes that even I get confused between them at times, as they are used interchangeably depending on where you are in Italy. All are usually served with heavier sauces, with some of the most famous dishes being fettuccine Alfredo, tagliatelle Bolognese, and pappardelle with meaty ragù. For these shapes, I recommend a rich egg-based dough or even yolk-only dough that's rolled to about 1.5 millimeters thick to retain a bite. Lightly flour the pasta sheet with semolina to help you handle the dough. This creates a coarse texture that can pick up the meatier, creamier sauces that usually accompany this nested pasta.

Keep Finer Strands Smooth

Nested pasta is of course not limited to the "holy trinity" and encapsulates many shapes. On the thinner end of the scale, you will find tagliolini and capelli d'angelo (angel hair). Here, the pasta sheet needs to be smoother and more pliable, so a yolk-based dough is recommended. This is because you have to cut the strands very finely, making the dough more likely to crack. Strand sizes should be around 1 millimeter wide for angel hair and 5 millimeters for tagliolini. Tagliolini is usually dressed with rich sauces of butter, cheese, and even truffle, whereas angel hair is served in broths or lighter sauces.

 28

Make Sure Your Filled Pasta Doesn't Snap, Crack, or Pop

The filled pasta category is so broad and so vast that first I want to explain a few simple rules for this behemoth. Having existed since the fourteenth century as delicacies for special occasions, filled pasta more than any other category is defined by its hyperlocality and family traditions. But there are some shared traits among the different varieties. First, the majority of filled pasta is made from fresh egg dough, though there are some exceptions, like Sardinian culurgiornes. The second is that the pasta sheet you work from has to be silky and smooth. These two elements help you avoid cracks or splits in the dough and allow the filling to shine. The smooth dough must enclose the filling and be sealed without air bubbles or your parcels will burst in boiling water and ruin the whole dish. So, whatever filled pasta you're preparing, make sure you have a smooth dough that is firm enough to contain your meats, vegetables, and cheeses, but also thin enough to enhance the appearance of the filling in these shapes.

Be Aware of the Tortellini/Cappelletti Debate

If there's anything that encapsulates the tight parameters within which we Italians distinguish pasta, it's the age-old argument about what is considered tortellini and what is considered cappelletti. With both hailing from Emilia-Romagna—cappelletti from areas like Forli, Ravenna, and Cesena, tortellini from Modena and Bologna—tortellini and cappelletti are small belly button–shaped parcels pulled together from two edges of a small filled pasta. They are both commonly served with broth and can be stuffed with pork, veal, beef, and some mixture of cheese, eggs, and nutmeg. With so many similarities you might be wondering what, then, are the differences?

This is the fun part because trying to explain the differences will just as quickly have you contradicting yourself. Tortellini from Bologna are usually smaller and are supposedly quite distinct. The rules dictate that the filling needs to be pork-based and include a touch of mortadella, a lot of Parmigiano Reggiano, and be served in brodo (broth). Cappelletti, on the other hand, allows for a cheese-based filling and can be served with ragù. How much people stick to this is up for debate.

The second distinction is the shape of the pasta sheet. Both pastas are made from a circle or square pasta sheet about 3 to 4 centimeters wide on each side. Some say tortellini always comes from a round sheet, whereas cappelletti comes from a square, but I spent years training in Imola, Emilia-Romagna, and we made tortellini from a square sheet. Italians don't always follow their own rules.

Last, and perhaps most important, is how the two shapes are folded over to make their semirounded parcel form. Tortellini is brought together around the pinkie finger leaving a small hole in the middle, whereas cappelletti is joined by simply uniting both ends—and they are slightly chunkier in general.

 30

Garganelli: Keep It Pliable but Firm

Garganelli is a ridged penne-like pasta shape typical in Emilia-Romagna, except that it's hand-rolled rather than extruded and has a seam. I would also argue that it's sturdier than penne and made to stand up against the meaty sauces it's usually served with. One legend says that it was first formed at Cardinal Bentivoglio D'Aragona's home in the early eighteenth century when the chef ran out of filling for cappelletti pasta and had to quickly invent a new shape with leftover pasta dough; others maintain that it was invented by the cook of Caterina Sforza, Countess of Forli, after a cat ate the filling for her cappelletti. Either way, a quick-thinking chef created a new shape by rolling short sheets of pasta on a weaving tool, the basis for what we know today as the garganelli board, which is a pasta comb made with wood and jute string (though most people just use a wooden gnocchi board).

Because garganelli is served with heavier dishes, I recommend creating a robust dough that is pliable and firm so that when cooked it retains its ridged tubular shape and doesn't flatten. To do this, use a yolk-only dough (or a mix of eggs with additional yolks) made with half 00 flour and half semola rimacinata. A gnocchi board or garganelli comb is necessary here; you take a small square sheet and roll it around a wooden stick diagonally from the sheet's corner against the indents of the board.

Farfalle: Don't Make It Too Chunky

This shape has become popular for its bow tie form and is used for a vast range of dishes, but it began its life in the fifteenth century as offcuts from cappelletti. Farfalle is so old that it predates the bow tie—its name actually means "butterflies."

It's fun to make farfalle. For the dough, use the egg-based recipe (see Rule 18), flatten, and cut into rectangular shapes of roughly 5 to 6 centimeters. I recommend keeping the sheet under 1.5 millimeters thick so that your shape doesn't become too chunky when you fold the middle, which can lead to uneven cooking. To create the folds, cut a rectangular shape (either with a knife or ridged pastry wheel) and pinch it in the middle.

Farfalle is often served with creamy dishes, so its little claw catches the flavor. I'm still a fan of farfalle al salmone, a creamy salmon dish reminiscent of the '80s that always hits the spot, but this shape pretty much works for everything.

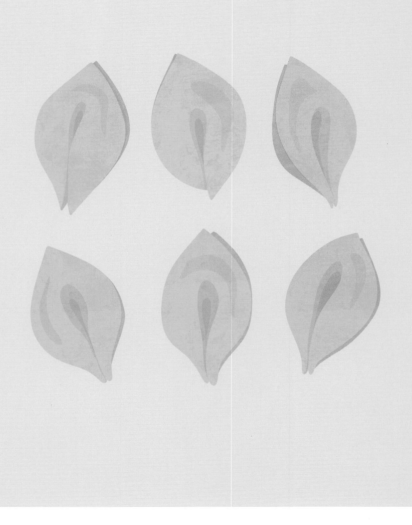

32

Sorpresine: Cheat with Style

A delicate, almost petal-like shape that looks like tortellini with its filling missing, *sorpresine* means "little surprises," but the surprise here is something you don't get—the filling. Sorpresine is one of a couple of names given to this pasta shape, the other being *inganna-preti*, which means "to deceive the priest." The name reflects the tongue-in-cheek humor of Romagna's peasant population of past centuries who were cracking a joke against their tax-collecting priests. These were people who probably couldn't afford the ingredients of the filling and had to make do with something more simple. *Strozzapreti*, which means "to strangle the priest," is another example of this dark humor.

Despite the colorful backstory, sorpresine is quite simple in reality. It's a sheet of squared egg pasta folded twice: first bringing together the tips of two diagonal edges, then the others. You pretty much follow the steps of tortellini without the filling. It can be served in broth or dry with tomato-based sauces. It's a good vehicle for thicker sauces—like many pasta types tend to be in Emilia-Romagna.

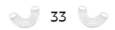 33

Know Your Trofie From Your Strozzapreti

Trofie is a roughly 3- to 4-centimeter corkscrew-shaped pasta that is made from a nugget of flour and water dough. Strozzapreti are twisted sticks about 5 to 6 centimeters long and made from a sheet of flour and water dough. The two are often confused with one another but there are some subtle differences.

Trofie is created by rolling a nugget with the palm of your hand until it becomes elongated and then running the side of your hand across the length of the shape in a diagonal motion until it becomes twisted. Hailing from Liguria, in the northwest of Italy, this shape is most often served with vibrant fresh basil pesto from the area. Sometimes the trofie is served with boiled potatoes and French beans, but this shape is now popular all over Italy and served with many different types of sauces.

Strozzapreti is also from the north in Emilia-Romagna, but here you create a sheet of pasta and cut it into strips, almost like pappardelle. Once you have a strip, you lay the top of it flat on your palm and use the other hand to rub along the dough to create a twist. Then you split off the twisted section and start again. Both shapes are very popular in Italy and go well with many sauces.

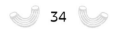

34

Learn the Basics of Flour and Water Pasta with Cavatelli

Cavatelli is a concave nugget of dough that acts as an excellent entry point into all pasta-making. It doesn't get easier than putting together some flour and water, picking up a morsel from the resulting dough, shaping it by hand, and tossing it into some boiling water. Cavatelli doesn't even have to be particularly equal or specific in size; just choose a rough dimension and get working by pressing your thumb or index and middle finger into the nugget and pulling it toward you. Some of the fondest memories of my young family are of us making cavatelli with our kids.

Cavatelli is a generic name that covers a host of localized pasta from central and southern Italy. Calabrians call it cavateddi and they create the shape only using an index finger. In Apulia there is capunti, formed by dragging the forefinger and index finger across a surface. In some areas, you'll find it served with heavier tomato-based sauces and meats; in others, usually deeper in the south, it's more often served with olive oil, vegetables, and even fish.

There is a reference to cavatelli as far back as the twelfth century, when it was called croseti and supposedly a favorite of King Frederick II of Naples. But as with all Italian legends, we'll take it with a grain of salt.

35

Gnocchetti Sardi: Be More Precise Than with Cavatelli

It's worth pointing to a shape that is very similar to cavatelli, but special all on its own. Gnocchetti Sardi, sometimes known as malloreddus, is a specialty in Sardinia that is shaped like cavatelli but is no more than 2 centimeters long and grooved on a wooden paddle to create a pretty ridged texture on the outside. *Gnocchetti sardi*'s literal translation is "little Sardinian gnocchi," and it is served with rich tomato sauces, ragù, greens, meats, fresh herbs, and/or fish. Likely the oldest form of pasta in Sardinia, gnocchetti Sardi is made from semolina rimacinata and water, and it has been served on special occasions such as holidays, festivals, and weddings for centuries.

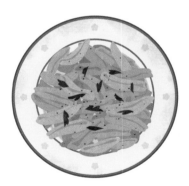

Master the Drag with Orecchiette

Orecchiette, the famous ear-shaped pasta nugget, is not easy to master, especially if you have to make more than one portion. I'm speaking from experience: Though I have made a lot of pasta in my life, to this day it takes me a long time to whip up a few portions of orecchiette, because it's hard to get accustomed to. You may have seen videos of women on the Strada Arco Basso in Bari, churning the cute little circles out like it's nothing. Some of them will make orecchiette all day long and sell them out of their home. They are so skilled and make it look so easy.

The process of making orecchiette is very similar to cavatelli, but instead of pressing the nugget with your thumb, you use a butter or palette knife to form it. You drag the knife toward you over the nuggets and press down with your finger on the other side to give the dough its circular, cupped shape. It may take a few tries to get it right, so take your time and enjoy the process.

The most famous orecchiette recipe is orecchiette con le cime di rapa, a dish made with blanched turnip tops, garlic, and breadcrumbs. But tomato-based sauces like orecchiette con ragù di braciola are also common for Sunday dinner—a richer dish with beef or veal meat.

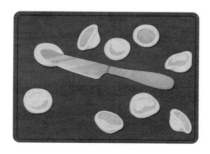

 37

Quadrucci, Filini, and Grattini: Make Them Spoonable

There are many tiny pasta shapes out there that work great in broth, but these three are my favorites. The thing to remember about these shapes is that they should be small enough to eat with a spoon. All three are made from egg-based dough but treated differently to form their distinct shapes.

Grattini translates as "finely grated"; it's made from egg and 00 flour dough that is shredded with a generic grater to create little pieces. Some may use a food processor to create the little shreds, but there's no hard rule here: The pieces can be jagged and nonuniform. I usually serve this to my kids with broth because it's so comforting and it's also an excuse to eat it myself.

Quadrucci and filini are both made from traditional sheeted pasta, but quadrucci are cut into small squares, little enough to fit a handful on a spoon. You can cut them up, let them dry out a bit, and either use them right away or store them in a resealable plastic bag and freeze them for later use. The filini, which means "little threads," are sliced very thinly from a sheet and the same applies.

 38

The First Rule for Maltagliati Is That There Are No Rules

Maltagliati are not so much a shape as an assortment of misfits. The literal translation for this pasta is "bad cuts." It doesn't matter if they aren't all the same shape, so long as they share a similar thickness to cook evenly.

I particularly love maltagliati because of their inherent versatility. When you make pasta, trimmings will always remain, especially when working with exact shapes like ravioli and tortellini. So what families for generations have been doing is using trimmings or offcuts from the dishes they are making as best as they can. Maltagliati can be square, rectangular, or simply wonky. The aim has always been to reduce waste, and in this, they have become a popular shape all on their own. I always have them in hearty soups, pasta e fagioli, pasta e ceci, or pasta e patate. Unusually, this shape can be made from either water and flour pasta or egg-based pasta.

Pici: Keep in Mind the Outsider of the North

Pici, the long strings of pasta thicker than spaghetti, are in many ways an outlier. Hailing from Tuscany in the north of Italy, they are made from eggless dough, which is uncommon. But rather than semolina and water like in the south, 0 flour—which is less refined than 00 flour—is used.

The way pici are made is also an anomaly. They are rolled from a strip cut out of flattened dough but almost pulled as they are rolled—a technique more commonly used with rice noodles in parts of Asia. The process makes them stand out from the majority of pasta. When making pici, ensure the diameter is no thicker than 3 millimeters and the length is 20 centimeters (about 8 inches) max.

These strings of deliciousness are commonly served with cacio e pepe, or as pici all'aglione, which is tossed in a tomato sauce with sweet, softly cooked garlic.

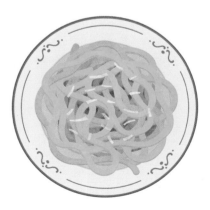

40

Be Patient with Fregula, the Couscous of Italy

Born in Sardinia, a region influenced by all sides of the Mediterranean, fregula is almost like a large couscous. It's made by adding small portions of liquid (often a mix of water, eggs, salt, and sometimes saffron) to semola flour and rubbing in a circular motion to create a crumb-like texture. As the mixture is rubbed together, you add the ingredients bit by bit until the balls are just under 1 centimeter. The fregula is then toasted and either boiled and mixed with a sauce or cooked like risotto. Technically a pastina, fregula also stands on its own as a quirky pasta shape that requires skill and patience to get right. Cooked in the traditions of the south, fregula dishes are often found with fish and vegetables, the most classic being fregula with clams or mussels and tomato sauce.

Su Filindeu: Get to Know the World's Rarest Pasta

I'm going to cheat here because the likelihood of you making su filindeu at home is slim. Only a couple of handfuls of families from Sardinia know how to make this special shape of pasta, the texture of which looks like a fine netting. Su filindeu, which translates to "threads of God," is all about its intricate process. The families that know how to make it will stretch the dough into threads by hand and after eight rounds of layering make over 250 delicate strands that are laid over a wooden frame and dried in the sun. The labor-intensive effort, combined with the rarity of the pasta, means that you can pay up to 70 euro for a pack of 1 kilogram of this very special pasta—if you are lucky enough to lay your hands on it at all.

The pasta is the star of the show in su filindeu dishes, and it is commonly served in a humble lamb broth with pecorino cheese. It's widely reserved for special occasions in the little town of Nuoro, the only place where the pasta is made.

 42

Store Pasta with Care

Once dough is shaped you can use it straightaway or decide how to store it depending on the specific shape you have made. You can store fresh pasta in the fridge for a couple of days (Rule 6), but as I like to plan ahead, I prefer to freeze pasta to retain its characteristics. You can freeze pasta for up to six months if it's not filled, and three months if it is.

A more traditional way to store pasta is to let it dry and then pack it into boxes or bags. To do so, flour pasta and leave it in a cool, dry place with a tea towel placed over it, turning the pieces now and then. The drying period can take as long as 36 hours for some pasta. This method requires a little more attention and does not work with filled pasta like ravioli.

Here are a few rules to apply to different varieties:

- **Lasagna:** Either dry on a tray and place the sheets in large resealable plastic bags, or keep the fresh sheets between parchment paper so they don't stick together and freeze as they are.

- **Tagliatelle:** Make sure the strands are well floured and not sticking when creating a nest, and either freeze them in an airtight container or leave them out to dry completely, then seal in an airtight container or resealable plastic bags.

- **Ravioli:** Lay the parcels out on a tray with parchment and don't stack them on top of one another or the humidity of the filling will make them stick. If the ravioli size is large and the filling very creamy, I blanch them in boiling water for 30 seconds to pasteurize them before freezing to extend their life and integrity.

DON'T JUST BOIL IT

The cooking of pasta is criminally underconsidered outside Italy. Many will think, *So what? It's just throwing some pasta into boiling water for 10 minutes, right?* Wrong. Cooking your pasta is a pivotal point for any dish. It's not just about softening pasta to the point of edibility; it's about bringing the best out of it. With the right techniques, you can enhance the flavor, texture, and overall appearance of an entire dish.

Many people's excuse for speeding through pasta cooking is, of course, saving time, whether it's restaurants precooking pasta so they can churn out more dishes, or home cooks looking to cut corners at the end of a long workday. But I want to stress that this is the point at which all of your work comes together: There is no sense in taking the time to make fresh pasta and drum up a beautiful pasta sauce if you're not going to give it the finish it deserves.

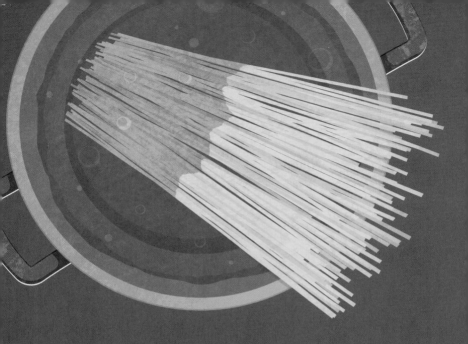

The rules I outline below are the result of many years of trial and error made by the Italian people. Some may be newer, while some are very old indeed. Once you have put these rules into practice, you'll wonder why you cooked pasta any other way.

A Healthy Amount of Water Leads to Best Results

A good rule of thumb when it comes to filling your pot is to use 1 quart of water for every 100 grams of pasta. It sounds like a lot, but it helps to achieve a consistent result, whether you're cooking for 1, 10, or 20 people. Having the right amount of water makes it easy to freely stir the pasta in the pot after it has expanded and enables uniform cooking. It also controls the water's boiling point better, returning it quickly to a rolling boil after the pasta has been added.

For those with environmental concerns, there are ways to reuse leftover pasta water. People have gotten creative over the years, using excess water in baking, gardening (mind the salt), and even for footbaths. My mamma taught me to always keep my pasta water to wash dishes. Simply let them soak in it and you'll be surprised—the starch released in the water is a great degreaser.

Boiling Water Is Best

It's important to drop pasta in the water when it is visibly boiling. This ensures that the starch starts cooking instantly, so the pasta absorbs less water and at a slower pace. It makes sticky pasta less likely, a little bit like when you sear and seal meat. When pasta is added to water that isn't boiling yet, it's a lot more likely to get mushy and harder to achieve that much-desired al dente bite as it will absorb more water. To reduce the likelihood of pasta sticking, stir as soon as the pasta is dropped in the pot.

DANILO SAYS . . .

As with all Italian rules of cooking, there are exceptions. Stirring immediately is important for most pasta shapes but can be disruptive for long pasta like spaghetti as there is a risk of snapping. In these cases, allow the pasta to soak until it's soft enough to be stirred.

Skip the Oil

It's a mystery as to who first decided to add oil to pasta water. It is uncommon, if not nonexistent, in Italy and one of the biggest misconceptions about pasta cooking there is. The consensus among people who do this is that the practice prevents pasta from sticking and it stops the water from boiling over the pot when the stove gets too hot. But there are already ways to prevent this: Using plenty of water stops pasta from sticking and the temperature should never be so high for so long that your pot boils over. In my opinion, putting oil in pasta is at best a waste of good oil and at worst it works against your dish. The oil binds to pasta and prevents the sauce from clinging to it, stopping it from adequately dressing and flavoring it. It interrupts those all-important starches from doing their job.

Great Flavors Are Built in Layers

Seasoning water with salt is the first step in seasoning the pasta itself. Try to think of your dish in stages, and season every component individually to build layers of flavor. When boiling pasta, reflect on the sauce you're likely to use: Will it have a briny dressing, or are there anchovies, clam juice, or capers? These ingredients will mean you need less salt in your water.

Many people become fixated on the type of salt needed for cooking pasta. Italians generally lean on rock salt for seasoning pasta water, and it's what I tend to use, too. It's less refined and more practical than table salt. With rock salt, I know that for 4 to 5 quarts of water I can use a small palmful of grains. This is harder to measure with table salt.

On the topic of flavor, the reason most people don't add salt while the pasta water is cold is that it's said to add a metallic taste to dishes.

Salt Your Water, but Not Like the Sea

"Salt your pasta water like the sea" has become a common adage. This has a place because it encourages people to salt more vigorously than they might initially intend, which can help build flavor. But I think this phrase is a little over-the-top. I would argue that pasta water should be seasoned like sauce: enough to genuinely add flavor. As a measurement, about 8 grams (a loaded teaspoon) for every quart is about right.

Add salt just before dropping in the pasta or the water can become too salty as it reduces from boiling. Don't be afraid to taste the water as you go along and add more water or salt as needed. But it's also never too late—if you accidentally find yourself daydreaming halfway through boiling and missing a step, just drop the salt in when you can.

Cook Fresh Pasta with Care

Fresh egg pasta cooks as quickly as 2 to 3 minutes, while semolina dough tends to take 5 to 6 minutes. All of this can change depending on the size and thickness of the pasta: A large shape like paccheri can take up to 15 minutes to cook, while spaghetti can take 8. This makes it more difficult to find the point at which the pasta is cooked perfectly al dente.

The white line rule doesn't work here, so the best way to know when to pull the pasta out is to taste test it. I usually just feel for a little bit of resistance in the bite. Be mindful of overcooking, as it's very easy for the pasta to get mushy with egg-based shapes, and chewy with semolina-based shapes.

Keep It Al Dente

In Italy, we believe pasta needs to be al dente to be enjoyed fully. *Al dente* translates as "to the tooth," which means that the pasta we cook should retain some bite rather than becoming mushy or chewy. It shouldn't crunch, but it should have a bit of resistance.

If pasta is coming from a bag or a box, a good way to identify if it's al dente and not too raw is to cut a bit of cooking pasta and look in the middle to see if there is a white line. If there is, it means the pasta is still too raw to be eaten and will usually need a couple more minutes of cooking to be just right.

With dried pasta, follow the instructions but subtract 2 minutes from the suggested cooking time. This is so you can taste test to see if you're happy with the texture while taking into consideration that the pasta will cook more when it's stirred into a sauce. It's standard practice in Italy to finish the cooking of pasta in the sauce by tossing it in a little early and allowing the pasta and sauce to meld.

Remember that different pasta shapes have different cooking times. Even the same variety can cook differently depending on the brand. And of course, the times are cut dramatically shorter when cooking fresh pasta.

DANILO SAYS . . .

If you are a beginner, don't be afraid to use a timer. It can be overwhelming to cook across multiple pots, so there's no need to rely on instinct. Just set a timer to the instructed time, barring 2 minutes.

Take Extra Care with Frozen Pasta

Fresh pasta that has been frozen takes a little consideration. Some will attempt to thaw the pasta before putting it in the water, but it's also fine to toss the fully frozen pasta into boiling water. There are just some factors to remember with both. Thawing will take up quite a bit of space as there needs to be some distance between the pasta shapes so they don't stick together as they defrost. There's also no guarantee that they will defrost evenly, and sometimes the frozen crystals can make your pasta mushy. On the other end of the spectrum, frozen pasta will require even more water than packaged or fresh pasta and needs very high heat. You'll also have to add a couple more minutes of cooking time than you would with fresh pasta and remember to taste test along the way.

A separate mention is needed for filled pasta here. Tossing filled pasta that has been frozen straight into boiling water is unwise because it's important to ensure that the filling is properly cooked. In a bid to do this, you may find that the pasta itself is overcooked. The last thing anyone wants is stone-cold filling on the inside and mushy pasta on the outside. To ensure uniformity I lay out filled shapes like ravioli on a baking sheet lined with parchment paper, leaving space between them, then I dust some semolina over them, and let them thaw. Then I drop them gently into boiling water. You may find that the pieces stick to the paper occasionally; if they do just throw them in with the paper and remove it with tongs.

Drain but Don't Dry

This might sound straightforward, but I see many people making mistakes
when it comes to draining their pasta. It's simple: Drain enough water so
you don't have soggy pasta, but don't allow pasta to sit and dry out. I don't
even drain the pasta over the sink, instead, I use tongs or a spider (a basket
skimmer) to pull the pasta from the pot and drop it straight into the sauce.
Letting pasta stand without water for too long will lead to chewy and sticky
pasta, so always cook it as close as possible to when you're going to serve it.

Don't Rinse Pasta (99 Percent of the Time)

Unlike with rice, pasta does not need to be rinsed. In this case, we're doing everything in our power to retain the starch and use it for a better sauce. Once pasta is boiled, don't be tempted to oil it either as it will do the same thing as when you put oil in water, preventing the sauce from sticking to the pasta and adding flavor.

One scenario does exist where rinsing and oiling pasta is acceptable: pasta salad. We enjoy pasta salad in Italy, too, particularly in the warmer months. In this case, rinse pasta in cold or ice water to quickly stop the cooking, and dress it with oil and other fresh ingredients like tomatoes, vegetables, or anything else you enjoy.

Don't Throw Out the Water!

If like me you spend time on social media, you must have heard every other food creator preaching about how you should save your pasta water. And while I couldn't hold it against you to be fed up with it, it does hold. You need the pasta water because you need the starch. Adding a bit of it to your sauce will help it cling to the pasta and coat it; it will help thicken it up to create an appealing texture and become richer in flavor. For thin dressings like cacio e pepe or aglio e olio, pasta water can bring the flavors together and give the dish that appetizing glossy look. Last, it can stop sauces from separating, creating an emulsion between the fats (oil, butter, cheese) and liquid (water, broth, sauce) to eliminate lumps and bind ingredients together. Just ladle some into a mug right before you drain your pasta—it can be a lifesaver.

Add Pasta to the Sauce
(Not the Other Way Around)

Every time I think of pale pasta sitting on a plate with a spoonful of sauce carelessly slopped on top, it brings me back to my first trips outside Italy or some inauthentic restaurants you'd find in tourist cities around thirty years ago.

This isn't about Italians being precious. The process of marrying sauce with pasta is not just a ritual but serves to create a better dish. Tossing strands of spaghetti or quills of penne into sauce helps to create the right texture; it incorporates air into the sauce to make it creamier (in Italy, we refer to this as *mantecare*). It's all about making your plate of food shine and creating an enjoyable experience.

A little advice would be to cook pasta when you have your sauce ready so you don't get overwhelmed and can focus on the final steps. After that, the world is your oyster: You can adjust the consistency of the sauce by adding some pasta water, or you can reduce it; you might want to add some extra-virgin olive oil or a knob of butter to give it some shine, or herbs to increase the flavor and depth.

Pasta Risottata: Add Water as You Go

This method could almost be called "one pot pasta," but in Italy, we call it *pasta risottata*—or pasta cooked like risotto. Especially good for thin sauces, this method entails tossing in your ingredients for the sauce and the uncooked pasta, then gradually adding water in the same pot until the pasta softens. This allows you to bind together the ingredients of a thin sauce with the starches in the water. Take aglio e olio: Normally the parsley, chile, and garlic would sit separately across your pasta, but this method results in a silkier texture and a better combined flavor. Now, like with risotto, this method takes a little more time than normal, and I wouldn't recommend it for all recipes as it has the potential to overwhelm already rich sauces. But it has some positive points as it creates fewer pots to wash and tossing everything into one pot always makes things feel easier.

Passive Pasta Cooking: A Rule for the Climate-Conscious

Recent years have had us all become a little more aware of energy waste, what that does to the environment, and what it does to our finances as energy prices soar. There is a method of pasta cooking that can save energy, and this is a method that resourceful Italians have used for decades when pressed for one reason or another. Here, you bring water to a boil, salt it, drop in your pasta, and allow it to cook for 2 minutes. Then you put a lid on, turn off the heat, and let it cook for the suggested time on the package instructions. The result can sometimes be slightly chewier than with the regular method, but if you're using quality pasta it will still work well enough.

MARRYING PASTA AND SAUCE

If pasta-making were a symphony, the saucing stage would be the crescendo. Up to here, the layers of preparation have been fairly technical: preparing the dough, shaping it, and cooking it. But this is where all the habits and quirky traditions of Italian families really emerge. As a result, it's also where you'll find some of the most divisive debates about the "correct" way to enjoy a dish: what ingredients can be paired together, which recipes are "authentically Italian," what should be used for toppings, and—*gasp*—whether you can use cream. It should come as no shock that I think many of these cultural ticks are too extreme—Italian households either don't follow them or bend them depending on the day and the situation. I think there should always be room for a little bit of freedom to create your own customs (without going too off track, of course—I am Italian, after all).

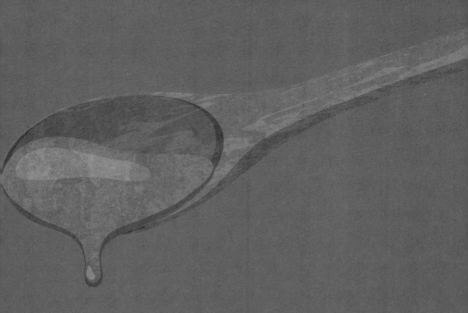

In this chapter, I will comment on some of the biggest taboos in Italian pasta cookery so you can make informed choices when making each dish. While I don't expect anyone to adhere to the strict preaching of Italy's most vehement traditionalists, it's useful to be able to follow the conversations around these dishes, even if it's merely to act like a local the next time you vacation or are invited into the home of an Italian.

Sauce Needs Adjustment

In Rule 54, we discussed how marrying the sauce and pasta is incredibly important for the overall finish of your dish. If you had to follow a single overarching rule for preparing all your sauces, I would make it this: With every activity—whether it's adding the pasta, topping with cheese or parsley, creating the base flavor, or incorporating a new quirky ingredient—always think about how everything will marry together to create a beautiful texture.

The way to do this is with constant adjustment, adding more pasta water if your sauce is looking too dry, incorporating fats to bind the sauce together, and even mixing and tossing the sauce to introduce some air and achieve that all-important mantecare (see Rule 54). Always add herbs and cheese off the heat, and do it at a level that enhances flavor, rather than distracts from it. And remember to taste, taste, taste. You'll find that finishing the pasta in this way is a constant adjustment—no one gets it perfect the first time.

Use Cream in Moderation

The use of cream in pasta sauces is a contentious issue in Italy. Up until the 1980s and early 1990s, it was used abundantly thanks to the influence of French fine dining, but it also became misused and overused. Cream had flooded day-to-day cooking and was being added in dishes that weren't traditionally meant to be rich. In reaction, a modern wave of chefs started making the correct argument that cream can overpower certain pasta sauces and overwhelm Italy's beautiful ingredients. This shifted the mood drastically to the opposite end of the scale, with many mercilessly antagonizing the use of cream in almost all pasta dishes.

As my nonna used to say, the truth is somewhere in the middle. Though a plate of maccheroni in pink sauce is at the top of my list of food nightmares, I believe that if used in moderation a glug of cream here and there doesn't hurt any dish and can actually play in its favor. Tortellini alla panna e parmigiano (cream and Parmigiano Reggiano) is a must when you visit Bologna, and farfalle panna e salmone (cream and smoked salmon) is a nostalgic classic that I prepare when I crave something creamy and old-fashioned.

Get to Know Which Fats Go with Which Dish (Then Forget It All Again)

Should your pasta sauce use oil or butter? This is another fraught debate that supposedly divides Italians between north and south—and then all Italians with the rest of the world.

Historically, people in the north of Italy would have relied on butter for flavoring their pasta because, as we have learned from previous chapters, the area is surrounded by the Alpine region, traditionally had great cattle, and was colder, so it made sense to find richer dishes with heavier sauces. Because it was known for its farming, the north also relied on lard for flavoring dishes. On the other hand, central and southern Italy are warmer, promoting the growth of the numerous olive trees that blanket the entire region. As a result, olive oil is the more readily available and natural choice for this region.

For a long time, these rules served a purpose: They were more convenient and appropriate for certain lifestyles. Today, with better transport, communication, and mass production, it's harder to say why dishes should remain a certain way—though, to no one's surprise, Italians still have strict rules for particular dishes.

DANILO SAYS . . .

It doesn't matter to me which fat you choose, but when you do use butter, I'd recommend unsalted butter for a creamier flavor that won't affect the seasoning of your sauce. For oil, I'd recommend an extra-virgin olive oil, but be kind to your wallet and apportion with care. I know it often sounds like Italians bathe in it, but we are master exaggerators by nature.

From my point of view, if you follow some general guidelines you should be able to avoid any major *passo falso*. Sauces with fish and vegetables tend to rely on olive oil, as many (including my family) believe that butter can overwhelm more delicate flavors. When it comes to olive oil, think of basil pesto, where extra-virgin olive oil is very much the costar, or spaghetti and clams. Butter is more commonly used for meaty or cheesy sauces, or ones that have a heartier flavor like mushroom- or pumpkin-based sauces.

Being a bit of a rebel, I would not judge you for swapping one over the other. Even some traditional recipes bend the rules, like butter and anchovy pasta from Rome, or meaty Genovese sauce from Naples, where beef and onions are caramelized in olive oil.

Fish and Cheese Don't Mix—or Do They?

What's the first thing you do with a hot bowl of spaghetti? The most Italian thing to do is sprinkle some grated cheese and start eating with abandon, right? It's a gesture we've all become familiar with, a ritual as old as time. But there is a breed of dish where it would be considered very controversial to garnish with cheese.

Conservative Italians will tell you there is one simple rule: Fish and cheese don't mix. Dusting a sauce that contains fish or seafood with a smattering of Parmigiano Reggiano or pecorino will have them clutching their pearls. In 2019, an Italian restaurateur in London even made headline news when he refused to serve cheese to a customer who requested it with their crab ravioli. A heated argument the two had on Tripadvisor caught much of Europe by surprise, while Italians cheered on their compatriot for bringing the customer to justice. Poor customer service in my book, but perhaps a bit of clever marketing for Italian rules and customs?

In principle, I agree with this rule, but I think there's more room to maneuver than is often presented. Just sixty or seventy years ago, mixing grated cheese with fish sauces was completely normal—many recipes of the time back this up. It was only after the 1970s when leading gastronomy figure Luigi Carnacina highlighted that strong cheeses tend to overpower

delicate fish and seafood. An excellent point, which has perhaps been turned into an overzealous witch hunt for anything that isn't considered an acceptable pairing.

I would never add grated cheese over a plate of silky spaghetti clams or a delicate crab and lemon angel hair, but I can't deny that many great combinations of cheese and fish can be created. It's about using milder cheeses that don't overpower the dish you intend to consume. My rule here is to play with different combinations and let your taste buds guide you, and I'm sure that you will find that some pairings work better than others.

Some pasta dishes support the use of cheese and fish: Take pasta with cozze (mussels) and pecorino from Puglia, or pesce spada (swordfish) with caciocavallo from Sicily. Or more recently there's the pairing of prawns with milky cheeses like burrata or ricotta that you can find everywhere (especially on social media). I love to make my pasta salad with marinated mackerel and buffalo mozzarella.

DANILO SAYS . . .

Maintaining a rigid rule like not mixing fish and cheese can be a good guiding point when you first start trying new recipes. As your confidence grows, you can begin being more playful with new combinations.

Become Acquainted with Key Italian Cheese Varieties

It could take years to truly learn every type of Italian cheese and where to use each. But breaking down a handful of the most common cheese types can cover a lot of ground, and besides, you have to start somewhere, right?

- **Parmigiano Reggiano and Grana Padano:** Parmigiano Reggiano and Grana Padano are the main cheese protagonists of Italian cuisine. Both are used across many recipes and sometimes even used interchangeably. Though similar in many aspects, their differences lie in the milk they are made from—with Parmigiano Reggiano coming from whole cow's milk and Grana Padano from semi-skimmed milk—and how long they are aged, with the former for 12 to 36 months and the latter 9 to 24 months.

    Staple ingredients in most Italian households, these cheeses are the bases of many popular recipes including lasagna, boscaiola (mushroom, tomato, and pancetta pasta), and even pesto. They have a milky flavor and go very well with robust meaty recipes, especially when using fresh egg or egg yolk pasta (there should be no surprise here as both cheeses are produced in the north of Italy).

- **Pecorino:** Pecorino is made with sheep's milk. It comes in different shapes, sizes, and ages and is produced all over central and south Italy in various styles. Roman pecorino (Pecorino Romano) is the key ingredient behind many renowned recipes like carbonara, amatriciana, and cacio e pepe, while Sardinian pecorino (Pecorino

Sardo) is a great addition to a bowl of malloreddus alla campidanese (Sardinian ridged pasta with pork ragù).

Depending on the area it comes from and the style of pecorino, this cheese can be used for more complex dishes ranging from lighter meat sauces to to stronger-tasting seafood like pasta con le sarde (sardines). Generally, it's a stronger, saltier cheese—something that's good to remember when cooking.

- **Ricotta Salata and Provola:** Two cheeses mainly confined to recipes from the south of Italy, ricotta salata and provola are fresher varieties that go well with a range of dishes from the area. Ricotta salata is a ricotta that's brined and dried for several weeks depending on the desired style. It has a milkier flavor than the cheeses we've already mentioned and goes well with sauces that contain lots of fresh vegetables like pasta alla Norma, with tomato sauce, basil, and fried eggplant.

  Provola, or provolone when it's a larger size, can be found in a variety of ages and sizes. Made from cow's milk, it can go from a few days of aging to a few months. It gives great body to sauces but has a low risk of overpowering flavor. It's great in spaghetti alla Nerano from Campania, a delicious pasta with loads of fried zucchini, basil, and olive oil and finished with copious freshly grated provolone that melts into a creamy consistency.

Go Cheese-Free on Occasion

In some cases, grated cheese can be swapped for toasted and flavored breadcrumbs, which we call *pangrattato*. These breadcrumbs are best with tomato-free recipes like spaghetti aglio e olio or orecchiette con le cime de rapa. Toss some savory, crunchy breadcrumbs over a dish, and just like that, Italian nonnas became the pioneers of vegan alternatives! I love my pangrattato toasted with olive oil, salt, lemon zest, and chopped parsley.

Chicken Can Be Paired with Pasta — Sometimes

Another taboo that ought to be broken: Italians do not add chicken to their pasta. There is nothing wrong with wanting to create a single meal with proteins and cereals served together—even Italians like convenience on occasion. You just won't find an Italian household sitting for dinner together with a plate of pale, dry spaghetti topped with a large piece of breaded chicken and maybe a bit of tomato sauce. Some may despair at this meal because it defies tradition; I despair because it's just not the best way to enjoy these two ingredients. Remember that the rule is to marry ingredients together: pasta and sauce, no matter what ingredients it may contain.

The problem is that the food extremists of Italy are shortsighted, having glorified Italian cuisine so much that they have themselves forgotten the many traditional local pasta recipes served with white meat and sauce. Some spectacular dishes with this combination come to mind immediately: tagliolini con i fegatini (chicken liver), a Tuscan dish deglazed with sweet wine from the region; tagliatelle al ragù di cortile (courtyard sauce), a tomato-free ragù served with chicken, duck, or rabbit; Sardinian lorighittas con sugo di gallo (cockerel sauce); or the finanziera sauce from Piedmont, where cockerel crests are slowly stewed with other giblets and vegetables. These dishes capture the correct interpretation of a chicken and pasta combination: a sauce where the chicken is sliced or diced and bound together with the pasta.

Balance the Use of Onion and Garlic

Onion or garlic—or both? Many will be wondering whether one ingredient is used more than the other when creating a good sauce. The truth is that both are the backbone of Italian pasta sauces and are commonly used interchangeably. Is there a clear rule that Italians do not mix the two? Not really. There is only the desire to limit the number of overpowering ingredients in each dish. Some may shy away from the combination, but onion and garlic can be found together in many soffrittos.

There is a subtle difference in their flavors. Garlic is pungent and if not dosed correctly can be overpowering. Onions share many similarities but can have a sharper flavor when served fresh and a sweeter flavor when cooked. For pasta sauces, they're usually chopped and cooked in either butter or olive oil over medium heat to become sweet and caramelized. A good onion base can save many sauces from tasting too acidic.

It would be difficult to offer a definitive case where garlic is the best choice over onion, and vice versa. Take a simple tomato sauce: Though it's more commonly created with garlic and olive oil, I've experienced it prepared with onion and butter, too, and it works just as well. As long as these ingredients are used in moderation, you can decide which route you want to take.

Choose the Best Way to Use Garlic for Your Dish

Though raw garlic can be incorporated into a dish, in most cases in Italy, garlic is cooked in extra-virgin olive oil—either chopped, crushed, or in camicia (cooked with the skin on). These applications are different for specific dishes: usually chopped for spaghetti and clams; crushed for penne all'arrabbiata; in camicia for pasta alla puttanesca. When garlic is used in camicia, it is often rubbed along the bottom of the pan, fried, and removed once cooked.

Garlic can burn easily at high temperatures, producing a bitter aftertaste if you are not careful. When shallow-frying garlic, I always recommend starting with a generous pour of cold oil that you cook over low heat until golden and caramelized. When cooked nice and slow, garlic becomes a lovely mellow, soft, and fragrant addition to your dish rather than a pungent aroma.

Chiles and Peppers Have Their Place, Sparingly

Despite facilitating the global spice trade throughout the centuries, Italy's use of spices is minimal. The exception lies in black pepper and chile, which appear in many of our recipes. As a general rule, the south of Italy tends to rely more on chile—Calabria is famous worldwide for specialties like the spicy pork spread 'nduja, which can now be found in every other hipster restaurant—while the north uses more black pepper.

The traditionalists will say that spices overwhelm the real flavors in your sauce, which I agree with when they aren't used correctly. I have seen some supposedly traditional restaurants serve chili oil at the table with a large shake of pepper for every dish, which just doesn't do most dishes justice. But I do think there is a place for chile and pepper, like with arrabbiata, aglio e olio, carbonara, and cacio e pepe.

If you want to add a little chile to your dish, far be it from me to tell you not to. But I can offer you some guidance: Try to avoid the mix of black pepper and chile in a single dish and use chile mainly with tomato- or oil-based sauces, while reserving black pepper for richer dishes containing mushrooms, cheeses, and butter.

Meet Soffritto—You Will Need It

Soffritto is the chopped mix of onion, carrot, and celery that forms the base of multiple ragùs, sauces, soups, and stews all over Italy. *Soffritto*'s literal meaning is "underfried," describing the gentle nature by which it needs to be cooked and also its position in the pan while cooking. It's worth getting acquainted with soffritto and perfecting your technique, as you're likely to use it in a multitude of dishes. Local and regional variations abound across Italy depending on the dish in question; some may add garlic, others herbs like rosemary, or chopped pancetta for extra flavor. The widely accepted recipe calls for a ratio of 2 parts onion, 1 part celery, and 1 part carrot for the right balance of sweetness and flavor.

The mixture is so common in Italy that it is sold in packets in supermarkets. In the United States, you may find a similar product labeled "mirepoix." Forever resourceful, my mother just cuts up a couple of portions and freezes the mixture for easy use later.

Don't Be Afraid of Spaghetti and Meatballs

Many will say that the dish of spaghetti and meatballs as we know it today is a bastardization of classic Italian recipes once they were exported to North America. With that, I agree, for good or for bad: Spaghetti and meatballs is an Italian American creation made by Italian immigrants to the country in the eighteenth century. But while many will highlight this peculiarity as a point of derision toward our cousins across the Atlantic, I say you can also feel proud of its authentic Italian roots. Many Italian regions have traditional recipes where pasta and meatballs are served together, from Sicily to my home region of Abruzzo. Take Abruzzo's spaghetti alla teramana, a fresh chitarra pasta served with tiny, delicious meatballs the size of your fingernail. Is it possible this was the inspiration for the common American recipe that has simply become supersized? I wouldn't be surprised.

Watch the Temperature for Cacio e Pepe

Another global obsession from Rome: cacio e pepe. Made up of just three ingredients—pasta, pecorino, and black pepper—it is also somehow one of the most difficult dishes to get just right. The simplicity of its ingredients is deceptive, as spoiling just one element ruins it all; it is very easy to end up with a lumpy, gooey sauce. Its success relies on one factor: temperature. You boil the pasta until it's al dente (as described in Rule 48) and set aside some pasta water. After this, you toss the pasta in with the grated pecorino, freshly ground black pepper, and a glug of pasta water to emulsify with the melting cheese and create a sauce. The trick is that the water can't be boiling but also not too cold, which is a fine balance. When done right, the combination should result in a perfect creamy texture and a glossy look, without the use of cream.

70

Elevate Your Pasta and Vodka Sauce

Though it has become a social media darling, vodka sauce is near nonexistent in Italy. Italy's demand for wine far outweighs that for spirits, and after the dish saw an initial trendy boom in the 1980s and '90s, its appeal faded.

The origin of vodka sauce is a bit of a mystery, with multiple people from both sides of the Atlantic laying claim to its creation. One story comes from Bologna, where it is said a restaurant named Dante conjured the creamy sauce; another comes from Rome, where a chef supposedly wanted to help popularize vodka in Italy. Others say its birthplace was New York, with credit given to chef Luigi Franzese, who worked at Orsini Restaurant. The documentary *Disco Sauce: The True Story of Penne alla Vodka* investigates these theories and more.

No matter where it's served, vodka sauce is a silky, pink sauce with an acidic edge softened by cream. My tip is to pair vodka sauce with a rarer pasta type like paccheri instead of the customary penne to make it more exciting. I also recommend using canned tomatoes (San Marzano, if possible) with tomato paste added to impart depth and aroma before finishing with cream and a splash of vodka.

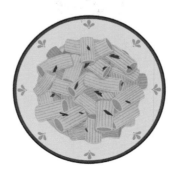

Experience the "New" Roman Carbonara

Carbonara is such a divisive dish that I include it in this book with hesitation. It is such a touchy subject among Romans, Italians in general, and even international lovers of the dish, that every time I have questioned any element of carbonara-making or dared to tweak the "traditional" recipe a little on social media, I get flooded with comments—many not so nice. The carbonara police are incredibly active, shouting people down, and yet, the cream-free recipe that they follow is likely no more than thirty years old. That's why I like to call it the "new Roman carbonara."

The origins of carbonara are very hard to trace; it has gone through many iterations. Historian Luca Cesari traces its appearance to the aftermath of WWII when American soldiers, with their penchant for eggs and bacon, influenced locals to create a combination with pasta. He even states that the first written recipe for carbonara was recorded in the United States. With that said, it's also clear that the custom of serving pasta with beaten eggs and cheese in Italy dates back way earlier than that. While it may not have been recorded by shepherds in the central regions of the country (my grandfather was one of them), many unwritten traditions have been passed down and we do indeed have a recipe for cacio e ova (cheese and eggs) that many equate to a meatless carbonara. Even during the 1960s, '70s, and '80s, carbonara included cream, pancetta, and cheeses such as Parmigiano Reggiano and Gruyère, which would be considered sacrilege now.

Today, this "new" Roman recipe is what most consider the classic. It is indeed delicious, but it involves only the use of pasta, eggs (sometimes yolks only), guanciale (cured pork jaws), Pecorino Romano, and a lot of black pepper. The egg must be creamy, the guanciale crispy, and the pecorino and pepper copious. If your lifestyle allows, it is worth experiencing this recipe in Rome at least once in your lifetime. A recipe is included in Rule 78.

 72

Get to Know a Pantry Classic: Aglio e Olio

Every Italian has had spaghetti aglio e olio on their plate at some point as a result of a rushed lunch or when in need of a late-night snack. A simple meal, aglio e olio is a spaghetti dish flavored with olive oil, garlic, chile, and parsley. There's not much to it—think of this dish as something that's easily thrown together when there's nothing else around. These ingredients are always lying about in an Italian pantry.

To make it, there are two separate schools of thought, from the traditionalists (of course!) and those that like their recipe creamier. The traditional way to make aglio e olio is to drain spaghetti well and almost fry it in garlicky oil, making the texture slightly sticky, and also adding chile and possibly pangrattato (see Rule 60). Others use the risottata method to create a more emulsified texture, adding water and pasta, and sometimes cheese with fresh chile, to create a simple but satisfying pasta dish in minutes. You don't have to be too rigid here—it's all about a quick meal. I have even made it when not entirely compos mentis after a few drinks.

Don't Be Shy About Making Pesto Convenient

When thinking of pesto, everyone's mind goes to the bright green hues of pesto alla Genovese, the basil, olive oil, cheese, and pine nut hero. But there are many regional variations of pesto: walnut pesto, red pesto with sun-dried tomatoes, and pesto alla Trapanese (pesto with almonds from Trapani, Sicily), and new and interesting recipes are popping up every day.

So, what makes pesto pesto? Two principles: Fresh ingredients must be mixed with olive oil, and the mixture pounded into a grainy paste. Of course, the food sticklers have much to say here, too. Those from Genoa will insist that there's only one way to make a pesto: by hand with a mortar and pestle using only local ingredients. But don't shy away from breaking tradition here; tossing all your ingredients into a food processor to create a creamy paste works just as well. Just pulse the processor in stages and stop when the texture is grainy and creamy—don't overdo it.

DANILO SAYS . . .

When making basil pesto, I load the food processor bowl with the ingredients, then chill in the fridge for 30 minutes. The cold will stop overheating in the processor, so it will stay green.

 74

Eat Fast Food, Italian-Style

Who said great food can't be quick? This is how I cook for my young kids when they're tired and screaming for food after a long day out. I place a pot of water on the stove at full power, sometimes with already warm/hot water from the tap, and close the lid. In 2 to 3 minutes it will be simmering and I'll add rock salt, wait a minute, then drop the pasta in. I put the lid back on, reduce the heat to medium, then remove the lid every once in a while to stir. Now it's time for the sauce: something quick like aglio e olio, the "real" Alfredo (see Rule 71), or pomodorini, a simple cherry tomato sauce. For pomodorini, place a pan on the stove to heat up while you wait for the water to boil, then sauté whole cloves of garlic in camicia (see Rule 65) in a drizzle of olive oil (this is no time for chopping!). Wait 2 minutes until it's golden. While you wait, halve a few cherry tomatoes and add them to the oil with a pinch of salt and a ladle of pasta water straight from the boiling pot so it softens the tomatoes with speed. In about 5 minutes the sauce will be ready and you can drain your pasta then add to the pan with a drizzle of oil, torn basil leaves, and a cheese of choice. And there you have it—a fresh Italian pasta meal in 15 minutes.

Learn the OG Italian Fettucine Alfredo Recipe

Believe it or not, fettuccine Alfredo is indeed Italian. One of the most popular Italian dishes in the United States, it has taken on a life of its own across the Atlantic while becoming almost nonexistent in Italy itself. So how did this happen? The story goes that fettucine Alfredo was created as a happy accident in the early 1900s by chef Alfredo di Lelio when he prepared the dish for his sickly wife. She enjoyed it so much that he eventually put it on the menu in his restaurant in Rome, Alfredo alla Scrofa, at which you can still order the dish today. This restaurant was visited by Hollywood couple Douglas Fairbanks and Mary Pickford during their honeymoon and they loved the dish so much they spread the word about it to all of their influential friends and named the chef "Alfredo the King of Noodles."

Naturally, the dish was eventually exported to the United States but has evolved over the years to include bolder notes, turning what began with simple butter and cheese into a white sauce with the addition of spices, chicken, prawns, and more. In Italy, it never became so popular, and the people who do still know it today see it as a simple dish to be prepared for kids or when one is feeling under the weather.

I like the original dish, but it is a stripped-down version of what you may know. In Italy we call this fettucine al burro (fettucine with butter). You simply cook your pasta al dente and save some water. Toss in the fettuccine with abundant soft butter and add splashes of (non-boiling) pasta water to emulsify, then add grated Parmigiano Reggiano and keep mixing until creamy. No cream or chicken is needed.

Double Carbs Are Not a Sin

Doubling up on carbs is not something Italians have ever been too concerned about because it's not something that occurs frequently in our cuisine, and even if it does our generally healthy Mediterranean diet means it doesn't become too much of a problem for the waistline. All this to say, it's not a massive *passo falso* if we find ourselves adding a carb to our pasta. There are a handful of traditional recipes that do this: pici with breadcrumbs from Tuscany being one of them, or pasta con la mollica, a similar recipe of long pasta that is topped with breadcrumbs from Calabria. Both are simple, delicious, and comforting. My favorite double-carb recipe hails from Campania, a wholesome mix of pasta, potatoes, and provola combined in a thick soup. The potatoes are cubed and stewed until soft, then the pasta is added and cooked through absorption of the remaining water and topped with cheese for a silky, rich texture—just gorgeous.

Try Vegan Recipes, as Made by Nonna

Tradition and veganism almost sound like opposites in Italian cuisine. It feels like an Italian nonna would have a lot to say about seitan, cashew cheese, and lab-made meats. But many traditional Italian recipes are vegan (without needing New Age substitutions) so long as you hold off on the Parmigiano Reggiano garnish. Pasta e ceci combines egg-free pasta with chickpeas in a creamy tomato broth, for example, and marinara is the world-famous tomato sauce made with basil, olive oil, garlic, and oregano, consumed for centuries. During World Wars I and II, Italians were so impoverished that meat and fish were a rarity, so legumes, vegetables, and herbs were the staple. Pasta e fagioli (pasta and beans) has long been a popular specialty in the country, as has minestrone with vegetables. The nonnas of today may or may not understand veganism, but they've been cooking vegan recipes for many years.

78

Prepare Easy Tomato Sauce, in the Way of South Italy

The quickest, easiest tomato sauce recipe comes from southern Italy. While the recipe is simple, its magic lies in high-quality ingredients. I like good, peeled San Marzano tomatoes with it because they aren't as watery as regular tomatoes. These help to create a chunkier sauce with juicy bits rather than a completely smooth finish. (With good-quality tomatoes, onion adds just the right amount of sweetness. If you're using a lower-quality tomato, you may need a pinch of sugar or baking soda to balance out acidity.) This is a versatile sauce that can be used with pizza and bruschetta as well as pasta.

Serves 4

3 tablespoons extra-virgin olive oil
1 tablespoon chopped onion
2 garlic cloves, crushed
750g very ripe fresh tomatoes or canned San Marzano tomatoes with their juices
Fine sea salt
1 tablespoon dried oregano
10 basil leaves (optional)
Freshly ground black pepper (optional)

Heat the olive oil in a large saucepan over low heat. Add the onion and garlic and gently cook, stirring occasionally, until golden, about 5 minutes.

Meanwhile, use your hands to carefully crush the tomatoes. Pour the crushed tomatoes into the pan with the onion and garlic, season with salt, and cook until slightly reduced, 25 to 30 minutes. Discard the garlic and season the sauce with the oregano and basil, if desired.

79

Danilo's Foolproof Carbonara

The "new Roman carbonara" is all about creating a smooth egg sauce.
No scrambled egg, no slimy uncooked whites, and no cheese lumps. This
foolproof method adds a step to a traditional recipe (used by many chefs),
but it helps you standardize the sauce process. Doing this takes away
the doubt of having uncooked eggs in your pasta dish and the fear of
scrambling your eggs into a pasta frittata because the heat is too strong.
It's easier than you'd think, and it works every time.

Serves 4

400g guanciale (or pancetta)
5 or 6 large egg yolks
2 large eggs
70g grated Pecorino Romano cheese
70g grated Grana Padano cheese
400g spaghetti or rigatoni
 Salt and freshly ground black pepper

Remove the rind from the guanciale. Slice the guanciale about 5 millimeters
(½ inch) thick, then cut it into thick strips or dice into cubes.

In a large skillet, gently cook the guanciale over low heat to slowly render
the fat until the guanciale crisps up to golden perfection, 10 to 15 minutes.
Using a slotted spoon, lift the guanciale from the fat, letting the excess
drain, and place it on a paper towel–lined plate. Reserve half the fat left in
the pan and discard the rest; set the pan aside.

Fill a large pot with water and bring it to a boil over high heat (this is for the
pasta). Salt the water right before you add the pasta (see Rule 47).

Meanwhile, fill a medium saucepan with a few inches of water and bring to a gentle simmer over low heat; do not let the water boil. In a heatproof bowl slightly smaller in diameter than the saucepan, whisk together the egg yolks, eggs, pecorino, and Grana Padano. Place the bowl over the simmering water to create a double boiler; the bottom of the bowl should not touch the water. While whisking, gently cook the egg mixture until it reaches a thick, custardlike consistency (or until it registers about 144°F on an instant-read thermometer), 2 to 3 minutes. Add some of the reserved guanciale fat for extra flavor and to give the sauce a nice shine.

Drop the spaghetti into the boiling water and cook, stirring occasionally, until al dente, following the instructions in Rule 48. Drain the spaghetti, making sure to reserve a mugful of the hot pasta water.

Transfer the spaghetti to the pan with the remaining guanciale fat and toss well to coat. Add the egg sauce to the spaghetti, then add a splash of the reserved pasta water to loosen it up and reach a creamy consistency. Stir and toss the spaghetti in the sauce to make sure it is well coated.

Add the crispy guanciale and season generously with pepper. Serve in large pasta bowls, topped with extra cheese.

MIND YOUR
MANNERS

It's no secret that we Italians are passionate about food. Everyone knows the cliché of an Italian, fingers pinched, loudly pontificating about why you should never break the spaghetti. While stereotypes like these can range from amusing to mildly annoying, from accurate to wildly inaccurate, I hold some affection for those who want to guard traditions. After all, the proliferation of Italian food culture around the world has also warped it to a point where it is often unrecognizable. The global Italian diaspora—aided by a large dose of commercialization—has created very different interpretations of what Italian food means to different countries. But can we call a mass-produced jar of tomato sauce sold by the millions a traditional recipe that's made with love? Or say that a dish doused in multiple processed cheeses and butters is an Italian delicacy when at home we use no more than a handful of fresh ingredients? Probably not.

While the quest for authenticity can be problematic and fraught with historical inaccuracies itself, there are some things that Italians living in Italy, or born in Italy, are convinced of. I'm hoping that the rules in this chapter, while far from comprehensive, will help you navigate a trip to Italy—or even a dinner party at an Italian friend's home—without receiving any bemused looks or stern words. They aren't *Il Galateo*, the 1558 "bible" of Italian etiquette with rules that continue to influence how many Italians think you should behave at a table. Most of those are stuffy directives that I wouldn't abide by myself, let alone expect a guest to follow. Instead, I offer you my selection of slightly quirky, sometimes silly customs we Italians live by that will make you feel at home the next time you're at one of our tables.

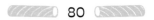

Don't Eat Pasta with a Spoon

Particularly when eating spaghetti, many wrongly believe using a spoon to help control the twirling of the pasta to be the height of elegance. I hate to break it to you, but to most Italians, it is not. Italians strongly believe that unless a minestra, creamy soup, or pastina in brodo is being consumed, a spoon has no place getting involved in pasta. Using a spoon for pasta, no matter the type, is seen at worst as bad manners, and at best as somewhat childish. That's why I'm including here this one rule from the *Il Galateo*.

Short pasta should be lifted with a fork, with each shape used as a scoop to collect more sauce from the plate. When consuming long pasta, it should be twirled with a fork using the curve of a plate for support. In the case of larger shapes such as rigatoni and paccheri, where getting the pasta on the fork might be more complicated, use the prongs to hook through the hole and scoop up the sauce.

DANILO SAYS . . .

I've seen plenty of Italians eating spaghetti with the help of a spoon, most of them from older generations. With that in mind, feel free to break the rule when you can't be bothered, or at least in the comfort of your own home. I will not judge you.

Cutting Is Cheating

Another habit that will have Italians accusing you of being a baby is cutting pasta with a knife. Unless it's a baked dish like lasagna, there is no reason to take a knife to your pasta: not for a bowl of spaghetti, a pot of paccheri, or a plate of farfalle. There is simply no excuse. Each pasta has been specifically shaped for a particular reason. It's what has been developed over the years for the best results, so why not follow through?

Don't Break Spaghetti

It's a rule you must have heard a thousand times but probably never quite understood. There's a boiling pot of water on the stove, it's been a long day, and you have 5 minutes until the kids start screaming—why wouldn't you just break the dried spaghetti so it easily fits in the pot?

Let's be frank: Breaking spaghetti is not going to change the flavor of a dish, nor does it somehow deform the inherent components of your pasta. It will work just fine. Italians steadfastly believe this because a long thread enables the pasta to be eaten how it was meant to be: perfectly twirled around a fork. Each spaghetti strand is cut to around 25 centimeters (about 10 inches) long so that it won't slip off or splatter sauce all over you at any moment. Quite simply, breaking the pasta makes eating spaghetti with tomato sauce, linguine with clams, or tagliatelle with Bolognese that much more difficult.

For many Italians, though, what makes the breaking of spaghetti so terrible is not so much the performance itself but the lack of effort to get it right. If so many people can learn to use chopsticks, why not learn to twist some noodles around a fork? And besides, if you're struggling with the twirl, it's probably better to opt for a shorter form that can easily be stabbed with a fork, rather than chopped-up bits of spaghetti—that's just inefficient.

There's also an easy way to ensure uniformity during cooking, without the need to snap. Simply twist the handful of spaghetti you are about to cook with both hands, then release it into the center of the pot. That way, the pasta will fall equally around the edges and avoid lumps as it cooks. Wait a few moments for the spaghetti to soften and then eventually push them down completely into the boiling water and stir.

This rule doesn't apply to all dishes, of course. There are always exceptions in Italian cuisine: We're not as strict as you might think. Certain regional soups like pasta with lentils or minestrone call for broken spaghetti, something Italians call spaghetti spezzati. You can even find it at the supermarket.

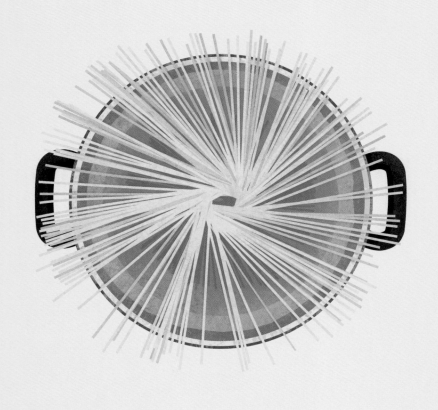

Pasta Is the Star of the Show

Finally, a rule even I will always abide by: Pasta must be allowed to shine. This means a pasta dish should never be eaten with a side. Many rules in this book are there to make pasta the star of the show; from choosing the right dough to the right shape and cooking technique. If a protein or fresh green is to be added, it should be well integrated so as to not overpower the pasta. Remember: When it comes to pasta it's all about marrying ingredients. Take gnocchi al radicchio: pasta with salad leaves that are chopped and cooked so that they become more united while maintaining pasta's primacy on the plate.

Naturally, pasta salads are the one dish where raw vegetables and herbs can be served fresh with pasta. This is because the focus here is on making the dish a salad, not a pasta dish.

Pasta Is a Primo Piatto

In Italy, traditionally you get an extra course on the menu: the *primo piatto*, reserved for pasta dishes and risotto only. Placed between the *antipasto* (appetizer) and the *secondo piatto* (main course), the extra dish ensures the proper dedication to pasta while guaranteeing that you savor the moment with friends and family.

Today Italian families try to abide by this order as much as possible, but as our days have gotten busier, along with the rest of the world, it's more commonly being confined to weekends and special occasions. On weekdays you're just as likely to find pasta served as a main course at lunch, accompanied by a light antipasto or side vegetable, then skipped at dinnertime when a meat, fish, or soup dish is served. Growing up I cannot recall a time when my mamma served pasta at dinner during the week, unless it was part of a minestrone.

The one benefit of having a primo piatto at lunch is that if you do happen to overdo it, then you have the rest of the day to digest before going to bed.

Learn the Ideal Portion Size for Pasta

Let's face it: Portion sizes have gotten larger all over the world, even in Italy (though some might try to deny it). Far be it from me to judge how much you put on a plate. Sometimes it's just good to know what has been done in the past so that we can review what we do today.

Traditionally, pasta portions were somewhere between 80 and 120 grams (3 to 4 ounces), depending on factors like shapes, types of dough, and sauces. In refined restaurants, where chefs worry more about the look of a plate, you may find smaller portions between 60 and 80 grams (2 to 3 ounces). At home, anything goes.

Things are different for fresh pasta, which naturally weighs more because of its water content and therefore can be slightly larger, maybe 150 to 180 grams (5½ to 6¼ ounces) for an abundant portion. The portion for ravioli, tortellini, and other filled pasta is approximately 150 grams, too, though this can be reduced if served in broth. It's an entirely different story

for gnocchi, as the general portion is above 200 grams (about 7 ounces)—sometimes even 250 grams (about 7¾ ounces)—simply because it weighs more when raw and will absorb less water compared to regular pasta.

As a final note, when weighing your pasta portion be mindful of the quantity of sauce you're adding. Though Italians enjoy well-dressed pasta, we don't drench it in the sauce. A good rule of thumb is for the weight of the sauce to be slightly under or equal to the weight of the pasta. If using a light, oily dressing made on the spot, you don't have to worry about weighing it.

Take Advantage of Every Bite With Scarpetta

While double carbs aren't taboo, you would certainly get some looks if you were to eat pasta with slices of bread at a restaurant. Italians love bread and have it aplenty with cured meats and cheeses, or together with our *secondo piatto*, but—to reiterate—pasta must be the star of the show. The reason for the rule here is quite simple: Pasta just doesn't go with bread very well. The textures clash, and the starches all fall on the tongue like a flat mush.

(If a chunk of bread with your pasta doesn't work, then why does the pici with breadcrumbs or the pasta con la mollica that we mentioned in Rule 76? It all goes back to the idea of pasta integrating with other ingredients to form the perfect bite. It's the same principle as with chicken in Rule 63: These ingredients should only be added to enhance the pasta experience and a chunk of bread on the side just doesn't do that.)

But there is one sneaky habitual case where you will find Italians pawing at the bread. Upon finishing a plate of tomatoey pasta, with plenty of sauce left on the plate, they may well clean the plate with a chunk of bread. This is called *scarpetta* ("little shoe"). Every Italian home cook would be proud to see you using a slice of bread as a sponge to sop up the leftover sauce on your plate—it's a sign of enjoyment at the Italian table. But be mindful: It isn't done when fine dining and you might want to avoid it if you care about making a good impression. For the record, I do not care about making a good impression and eat scarpetta wherever I go if I truly enjoy the dish.

Choose Quality over Quantity

Italians are incredibly invested in pasta quality, so much so that there's a law that ensures all packaged pasta in the country is made from durum wheat semolina to ensure that it is nutritionally dense with proteins and fibers.

Finding good commercial pasta brands internationally can be trickier, as there are no laws protecting it, like in Italy. On supermarket shelves, it's hard to tell what a premium pasta is and what is not, even when the label reads "'made with durum wheat semolina." Brands process the pasta in different ways. A low-quality brand, for example, will not use 100% semolina and the pasta can be dried at high temperatures to speed up the making process, reducing its nutritional value. In contrast, a premium brand will use higher-quality semolina at a higher ratio and dry it over a couple of days at a low controlled temperature (around 120°F), helping it retain its nutritional properties. If in doubt, choose a brand imported from Italy as even the most mass-produced pasta here has certain standards.

Whether it's made at home or you buy a good brand in the supermarket, choosing quality pasta ensures that it can be a part of a nutritionally balanced meal and not the blood pressure-raising, simple carb it is often demonized to be. And remember, the longer you cook pasta, the higher the glycemic index, so it's an extra reason to aim for al dente.

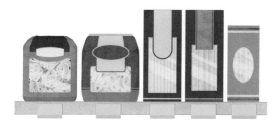

Eat Local, Eat Slow

If you're one of the lucky people planning a pilgrimage to Italy to taste all of its finest pasta, one rule will widely ensure you will get a good meal: Eat local. Italy has twenty regions, each with its specialties, and it would be a shame to order something that isn't suitable for the area you're visiting: It just won't be as good. So don't order cannoli in Emilia-Romagna or Bolognese in Sicily. Without a doubt, local food is the best food.

And while you're there, savor meals like an Italian. Apart from during busy weekday lunches in major cities, Italians tend to take their time with pasta, as with food in general. It's one of the primary sources of joy in this life. It's a perfect time to unwind, sip a glass of wine, and entertain interesting conversations. And, let's face it, not rushing your pasta is also good for digestion—and how you make sure there's room for dessert.

Be Aware of Drinks That Detract from Pasta

If you want to follow Italian traditions to a tee, drinks should marry with the flavor of your pasta just as much as the pasta marries with the sauce. Sugary drinks are rarely paired with meals in Italy because they detract from the flavor of the food. Sure, a soda with a pizza slice may be permissible occasionally. Still, given that you now know how seriously Italians take their pasta, it shouldn't come as a surprise that the combination upsets them.

Harvested from the same ground as other local ingredients, a nice glass of wine is the perfect accompaniment to pasta. I'm no wine expert, but what I recommend is to approach wine the same way you'd approach regional recipes as I have described them: Stick to what's local, and ask for a common regional pairing. Two typical pairings are tagliatelle alla Bolognese with a nice glass of Lambrusco (a fresh, sparkly red wine) or pasta alla Norma with an Etna Bianco (a mineral white wine from Mount Etna). If you don't drink, mineral water works, too.

DANILO SAYS . . .

Coffee is reserved for the end of a meal to help you digest and energize. It should by no means be had alongside pasta as it interferes with its mellow flavor. And whether it's lunch or dinner, this should always be a short, sharp espresso. Avoid cappuccino past noon if you want to avoid judgment; it is very much seen as a breakfast drink.

The Waiter Knows Best (90 Percent of the Time)

If you need help deciding whether to add pepper, chile, or cheese when a dish arrives at a restaurant, just play the waiting game and see what the server suggests. In Italy, staff will tell you how things are best served 90 percent of the time, taking the guesswork out of your decisions. If the server offers you grated pecorino or pepper with your pasta, take it as an opportunity to enhance your dish. If it wasn't offered, it probably just doesn't go that well with what you ordered.

Always Ask for a Second Helping

Every culture has customs that signify satisfaction from the dinner guest. In Japan, it may be slurping your noodles, in China, it's leaving a small bit of food on a plate, and in Italy, it's asking for a second portion.

For us Italians, the moments spent at the dinner table are the most important of the day. Elongating this period can only be viewed as a good thing, which is why if you ask for more pasta you're likely to be obliged and appreciated as a guest—especially as it's made in big batches. My mamma still loves it when I ask for a second round of her ravioli when I visit, and I'm not shy about asking in other homes, too. Of course, this custom does not apply in restaurants—unless you want to pay for more!

Learn Appropriate Dishes for Every Occasion

Hosting can be stressful, even if you love doing it. Having catered for many dinners across my career (including for world leaders and dignitaries), I can confidently say that pasta is the perfect choice for events and special occasions. It's easy to cook in batches, versatile, everybody loves it, and it's somehow still impressive on a plate, especially when made fresh. While a variety of pasta dishes can be used for every scenario, the following rules are suggestions for what recipes can work for different occasions.

Cook Something Special for Big Occasions

I, like most Italians, believe that there is no celebration without a sumptuous meal—and there is no sumptuous meal without pasta. Weddings, birthdays, anniversaries, graduations, and other important milestones are all worth celebrating with the act of eating.

The best pasta dish for celebrations should be something out of the ordinary, perhaps a luxurious ingredient you would not usually grant yourself, or a preparation that requires effort. Think of a silky plate of all-yolk tagliolini dressed in butter and served with fresh truffle or a plate of angel hair with crab. My personal favorite is egg yolk ravioli: a single-serve parcel with spinach and ricotta filling that encases a whole yolk. Cooked in boiled water to keep the yolk runny, the raviolo is served with copious grated cheese, freshly shaved truffle, and brown butter. Very special, indeed.

Avoid Long Pasta for Dinner Parties

What you serve at dinner parties is widely determined by party size and the time you have. But there are some general guidelines I follow to make it easier to decide on the perfect dish. In terms of shape, I try to avoid long pasta as it is more difficult to mix and dress in the pan, as well as to portion neatly on a plate. Also, it can be tricky for guests to eat it politely; if they aren't expert spaghetti twirlers, they will struggle with a plate of linguine and make a mess across the dinner table and over themselves. According to classic etiquette, the rule is to avoid dressings that are too oily or smelly. Red sauces stain, while green sauces like pesto tend to become discolored if left sitting in a pan for too long.

I love serving freshly made gnocchi for dinners, but a nice dry paccheri is also a good option and always makes a great impression because it is both uncommon and practical. The very best choice in my opinion, however, is a lasagna or pasta bake. While it does require a lot of work, it can be prepared ahead of time and baked as the guests arrive.

Impress a Date with Cocoa Pasta

All pasta is romantic in its own way, but to really impress a date you might want to push the boat out and get experimental. Now we know oysters, chocolate, crustaceans, and certain spices are considered aphrodisiacs, but few would have thought to combine these ingredients. In many cases, this is for good reason: oysters and chocolate? No, thank you. There is a fun combination that could work, however. I prepare cocoa pasta dough (unsweetened, of course), form it into tagliolini, and serve it with a spicy lobster sauce with fresh cherry tomatoes. Here you have it all in one dish: bitter notes from the cocoa, a zing from the tomatoes, sweetness from the lobster, and a kick from the chile. It makes for an impressive dish, especially when served with a glass of cold bubbles. And in the worst-case scenario, if the date goes wrong, at least you have a delicious pasta dish to enjoy.

Forgo the Spaghetti for the Kids

If you've ever watched a toddler eat spaghetti, you know it's the funniest thing to witness. But let me tell you something, the cleanup is not funny or cute. For kids, I tend to serve something with a grip, like farfalle, especially as they love the bow tie shape. For sauce, I will usually batch-cook my easy tomato sauce found in Rule 79, add mini meatballs, and freeze it in airtight containers ready for whenever they start screaming. Sometimes I will have it myself, as who doesn't love tiny meatballs? They're cute and tasty.

Simple Is Best for the In-Laws

This is as tricky as it gets, and for the single people out there, I would compare it to cooking for your boss. The first time you cook for the in-laws can be particularly nerve-racking. When preparing a pasta dish, you need something easy to manage both in the kitchen and at the table. Stay away from dressings that come together at the last moment, like cacio e pepe or carbonara, as they add too much pressure. Instead, prepare a sauce that can be cooked ahead of time and kept at stand by for serving, like an amatriciana.

Another tip is to avoid flashy, expensive ingredients. No one likes a show-off, at least not in the first meeting. Save the caviar pasta for when you know each other better. In my experience, the best way to impress older generations is to show that you put care into the preparation of your dish. Make something like fresh maltagliati egg pasta (see Rule 38) with a simple, tasty sauce that is satisfying even if not perfect. People will always appreciate the effort.

Soothe a Heartbreak with Mac and Cheese

In the throes of heartache, it's hard to find comfort. You might be a little sad, you might be a little disappointed, even angry, and what could be more soothing than mac and cheese? It's rich, it's tangy, and it's the ultimate act of self-love. But don't grab it from a package. Make something special—you deserve it. Add a combination of four cheeses like an Italian would do: Gorgonzola, Taleggio, provola, Grana Padano, Parmigiano Reggiano, or other rich and stinky cheeses that are going to right the world's wrongs. The gooier, the better.

Soothe a Hangover with a Poor Man's Carbonara

We have already discussed how spaghetti aglio e olio is great for a late-night snack, but I want to talk now about the pasta you need the morning after, in the thick of a hangover. It's past noon, you can't work out what you did last night, and you need to eat. Here's where you need something simple and bold. A short and easy-to-manage shape is best, as if you were cooking for the kids (but please use cutlery if you can); rigatoni and penne are great choices. In terms of sauce, you want something that resembles a carbonara but without the fuss. You are partially incapacitated after all. Pasta cacio e ova winks at carbonara, but in this case, the eggs are beaten with grated cheese, added to the pan with cooked pasta and garlicky oil, and fully cooked through until scrambled. This is all then served with a sprinkle of chile or black pepper. What you end up with might not be pretty, but it will help you return to the world of the living.

Cook Pasta e Fagioli the Week Before Payday

Pasta is inherently cheap, and along with rice, is one of the few staple ingredients that is affordable for people all around the world. There are more stories of Italians being resourceful with their pasta dishes than extravagant. Our cuisine is full of examples of how to turn humble ingredients into restaurant-worthy dishes. The choices are endless: pasta with mollica (stale bread), *spaghetti del poverello* (translated to "pasta for the poor"—pasta with a fried egg and pecorino), and pasta alla puttanesca (a simple sauce of tomatoes, black olives, capers, anchovies, onions, and garlic). But of all the many budget-friendly pasta dishes, I would choose pasta e fagioli (pasta and bean soup). Use whatever pasta you have on hand from open packages or maltagliati and add whatever herbs you have in the pantry with beans. A high-protein, perfect pasta on a budget.

Acknowledgments

Thank you to my pasta team: writer Kaltrina Bylykbashi, editor Caitlin Leffel, illustrator Rebecca Hollingsworth, designer Renée Bollier, and project editor Ivy McFadden.